MALE BODIES

HEALTH, CULTURE
AND IDENTITY

Jonathan Watson

OPEN UNIVERSITY PRESS
Buckingham · Philadelphia

Open University Press
Celtic Court
22 Ballmoor
Buckingham
MK18 1XW

e-mail: enquiries@openup.co.uk
world wide web: http://www.openup.co.uk

and
325 Chestnut Street
Philadelphia, PA 19106, USA

First Published 2000

A catalogue record of this book is available from the British Library

ISBN 0 335 19786 8 (hb)   0 335 19785 X (pb)

Library of Congress Cataloging-in-Publication Data
Watson, Jonathan, 1960–
    Male bodies : health, culture, and identity / Jonathan Watson.
        p.   cm.
    Includes bibliographical references and index.
    ISBN 0–335–19786–8 (hardbound). — ISBN 0–335–19785–X (pbk.)
    1. Men—Health and hygiene. 2. Body image. 3. Social medicine.
    4. Health behavior—Great Britain. 5. Men—Health and hygiene—
    Great Britain. I. Title.
    RA564.83.W38 1999
    613'.04234—dc21   99–29672
                                                                  CIP

Typeset by Graphicraft Limited, Hong Kong
Printed in Great Britain by Biddles Limited, Guildford and Kings Lynn

CONTENTS

ACKNOWLEDGEMENTS

Thanks are due to many people who helped make this book a reality. In particular, I owe a great deal to the men – and their families – who allowed me periodically to interrupt their lives over a two-year period and on whose experiences and perceptions this book is based. In all cases, I was received into their homes with courtesy, humour and interest and they talked openly about issues that were often deeply personal. If the research adds anything to our understanding of men's personal experiences of health, it will in large measure be because of this. Thanks are also due to those primary health care staff who generously allowed me to observe and ask questions about well man screening in their practices.

Over the course of the research that contributed to this book and in its writing several colleagues, notably Sarah Nettleton, Sarah Cunningham-Burley, Nick Watson, Kathryn Backett-Milburn, Stephen Platt and Sandy Whitelaw have debated ideas with me and provided helpful criticism. To them I owe a debt of gratitude. Robin Bunton manfully read the entire text and gave invaluable criticism. If I achieve any clarity in presenting this research it is, in large part, because of such comment. Any errors or omissions are mine alone.

At Open University Press I am grateful to Jacinta Evans for having the faith to take me on in the first place and to Justin Vaughan who took over as my editor early on and who demonstrated immense patience as I tried to juggle manuscript and work demands. Gaynor Clements always kept in touch, tactfully urging me on. Positive strokes do work, eventually.

I have also been given a great deal of practical assistance and this requires similar acknowledgement. The original research was supported by a National Health Service bursary from the Management Development Group of the Scottish Health Service and Grampian Health Board. Jane White, Karen Smith and Norma Bain heroically and accurately transcribed many hours of recorded interviews. Thanks are also due to Steve Garrard at the Health Education Board for Scotland for producing the illustrations and graphs, to the library staff for ferreting out 'lost' references and especially to Jackie King for retyping and formatting the manuscript.

A number of permissions require acknowledgement. The illustrations in Chapter 1 drew on data from a range of sources. These are specifically noted within the relevant figure caption but permission to use data from those sources is gratefully acknowledged here. Chapters 3 and 7 contain reworked parts of a paper originally published as Watson *et al.* (1996). Permission to reproduce Figure 3.1 was granted by the Department of Health. Permission for Figure 3.2 was kindly granted by the Leith Agency, the Edinburgh Club and Victor Albrow. Some of the concepts around bodies that are discussed in Chapters 3 and 4 were originally introduced in more abbreviated form in Watson (1998).

The biggest debt of thanks must be to my family, who have suffered my physical and emotional absences and yet supported me in ways and upon occasions too numerous to recount.

The views expressed are those of the author and not of the Health Education Board for Scotland.

INTRODUCTION

Consider the following two pieces of information about prostate cancer. First, a brief life history. Fraser was born in 1921 on a croft in Sutherland, in the far north of Scotland. A local woman assisted his mother in the birth, and when Fraser was born he weighed in at 9 pounds. A big boy, even by today's standards. He had a sister, and when they were young their parents moved to Glasgow, in part to be sure that their children would have a good education. They did. Fraser eventually became a high school teacher. Both children were self-reliant, with a dry sense of humour – so dry that if you blinked, or were English, you would miss the joke. Physically, Fraser was 5 foot 5 inches tall, had broad shoulders, hands like shovels, a handshake that could crush hands; he was naturally strong right into his last year. He had never suffered from serious illness and was stoical about the odd broken bone. At the age of 70 he was diagnosed as having prostate cancer, and unexpectedly died shortly afterwards. It is possible that, like many men, he presented to the doctor when the condition was too far advanced. More likely he had a heart attack or stroke, since friends and family assumed he had such strength of body and mind that he would try to fight the cancer.

Second, according to the publication *Cancer Registrations in Scotland: 1986–1995* (Information and Statistics Division (ISD) Scotland 1998a), cancer of the prostate was the third most frequent cancer to affect men in Scotland between 1986 and 1995. During this period the incidence of prostate cancer increased in Scotland by 48.8%. The disease is not very common before 50, but risk increases rapidly after that age. The ISD report states that this incidence trend had two components. First, a gradually increasing incidence up to 1991, possibly due to increasingly common incidental find-ings of small tumours in the prostate during surgery for benign prostatic hyperplasia. Second, a steep increase between 1992 and 1993, which might have been associated with the introduction of the prostate specific antigen test for diagnosis and disease monitoring. Deaths attributed to prostate cancer also increased during this period (ISD Scotland 1998a: 108).

Both the brief life history and the epidemiological analysis of prostate cancer are important and relevant forms of knowledge; both are ways of knowing about men's health. The first is individual, data-rich, complex and, you might argue, anecdotal. The second is based on aggregated data, gives a fairly precise picture of a condition, but is essentially reductionist; it misses the bigger picture.

Nevertheless, if we want to be sure that actions intended to improve health are appropriate and acceptable then we need to improve our under-standing of what creates good health and what processes can bring about improvements in health at different levels: individual, community, organ-ization and policy. Individual bits of research are important, but the pro-cess of distilling lessons, of sharing them and then making decisions, is also influenced by making connections between research findings (if available), professional practice, lay knowledge and theory. In effect, an evidence-based approach to health promotion or public health needs to recognize that different sources of knowledge inform policy and are required to turn policy into practice and assess the impact of such action (Hirschon-Weiss and Wittrock 1991; Chapman 1993; Ham *et al.* 1995; Research and Evalu-ation Division 1996; Speller *et al.* 1997; Tones 1997).

Looking at men's health, what is striking is the absence of knowledge grounded in the everyday experiences of men themselves. This may seem an illogical position, especially as men are so prominent in constructing and expounding upon the wider social, political and economic transformations that are affecting society at the end of the twentieth century. However, expanding on an argument presented elsewhere (Watson 1998), I will be suggesting that current medical and social debate around men's health is undermined and under-informed by a failure to explore men's perceptions of health and maleness as a personal, cultural and social phenomenon. In this sense, we need to differentiate between the production, reproduction and erosion of patriarchy as located within social structures and institutions, and masculinities as a personal and embodied response to and reflection of these social and cultural values.[1]

At a time when what it means to be a man and related civic values are being reappraised, dumped or repackaged, being male has been taken up as part of the political agenda of social transformation. One commentator has referred to the stripping out of 'the stable architecture of clear goals . . . consistent rules . . . and male virtues' (Daley 1998) that has shaped society's expectations of boys and men and through which they could be esteemed in their own right. Why should this matter, and how does it relate to personal experience of maleness and men's health experience? Arguably, because macro-level transformations have personal-level consequences, and as the latter accumulate so they may impact on the shaping and direction of the former. Hence, understanding of individual-level everyday experience illuminates the working-out of broader social forces. Health statistics are another marker of this dynamic, and recent statistics are depressing: in the United Kingdom women live five years longer than men (ISD Scotland 1998b); men aged 15–44 are nearly four times more likely to commit suicide (General Registrar Office for Scotland 1996); suicides by young men aged 15–24 have increased by 75% in the last ten years; men under 65 are three times more at risk of coronary heart disease (CHD) compared to women (ISD Scotland 1998b); and sexually transmitted infections (including HIV) occur mostly in men (ISD Scotland 1998b). Particular occupational groups such as farmers are at highest risk of death from suicide and fatal injuries at work (Anon. 1998). Confronted by such evidence, it has been argued that it is in the health interests of men 'to change, abandon or resist aspects of masculinity' (Sabo and Gordon 1995: 16).

Encompassing the elements of the evidence-based approach that I have described above, this book sets out to explore the basic premise behind Sabo and Gordon's challenge: that masculinity is intrinsically damaging to men's health. It does so by developing a theoretical and empirical exposition of an embodied approach to men's health. This approach suggests that embodied experience of masculinity is central to understanding the limits and potential of social, political and economic transformations on the individual. This thesis is itself grounded primarily in an analysis of the accounts of a particular group of men living in North East Scotland and aged between 30 and 40 as they struggled to cope with the competing expectations of work, family and friendship.

Chapter 1 sketches out some of the more orthodox evidence on the state of men's health, including the broad policy and practice context. This does not amount to an exhaustive review of all data sources – for two current reviews, see Department of Health (1993) and Lloyd (1996). Rather it shows how a scientific discourse on men's health has emerged. This is set within a broader context of the evolution of surveillance and the practices of governance in public health and the extent to which lay concepts of health are complicit in or resist such direction (Chapter 3). The latter part of Chapter 1 introduces and explores the concept of masculinity as an explanation for variations in health outcomes between the sexes. Chapter 2 presents a review and critique of the body and health as found primarily in 'sociology of the body' and more broadly within the humanities and medical literature. Chapter 3 starts by examining the debate around the relative status of scientific and lay knowledge. It goes on to present empirical data that demonstrate continuity with earlier studies into lay concepts of health but departs from these by exploring the bodily dimensions of such concepts. The embodied dimensions of lay knowledge in men have often been missing or perhaps latent in some of these previous studies, possibly reflecting an earlier presumption that the body could only be found in studies of the experience of chronic illness and disability or female embodment. Indeed, such work has maintained the body as a subject of study (Kleinman 1988; Martin 1989; Charmaz 1990; Helman 1990). By contrast, male embodiment has until recently not been adequately addressed in the social sciences (Connell 1995; Seidler 1997; Bloor *et al.* 1998; Higate 1998). Chapter 4 moves to an examination of embodied experience in everyday life and, more particularly, shows, through informant accounts, how personal and social identity is challenged and maintained. Chapter 5 addresses the concept of embodiment as a location for those practices that shape masculine identity. It then moves on from this conceptual framework to present a core analytical concept of *being in shape* – derived from a grounded analysis of informant accounts. This concept is then applied to an analysis and interpretation of informants' experience of a well man clinic in Chapter 6, illustrating the importance of individual agency in the context of surveillance and the practices of governance associated with primary care screening. Finally, conclusions and implications for action (practice, policy and research) to improve health are drawn out (Chapter 7).

In summary, Chapters 1, 2 and 5 delve into theory. Chapters 1, 3 and 4 present research findings from population survey data, epidemiological studies and qualitative research. Finally, Chapter 6 links theory back into practice.

Putting embodiment into play

Embodiment was not the original focus of the studies that inform this book, and this in turn has methodological implications for the ways in which the body can be approached to which I will return shortly. My first intention was to explore perspectives of health among men, drawing upon an established tradition of writing on lay perspectives. It is clear that current debate around men's health, and perhaps men's place in society, is crippled by the lack of attention paid to personal accounts and perceptions of maleness. The irony is that whilst we have moved towards a richer and subtler appreciation of women's health over the lifecourse, a reassessment founded partly in the context of lay experience, one might argue men have come to be defined, even constrained, both by their physiology and related behavioural characteristics. In this respect, Connell (1995: 45) notes that 'true masculinity' is almost always thought to proceed from men's bodies: 'the body drives and directs action' (aggression and sex feed off testosterone) or 'sets limits to action' (men do not naturally take care of young children).

Treated thus, the male body has a narrow and partial presence. Arguably the knowledge and understanding that flow from this contribute to normative constructions of the male body and behaviour which 'are disempowering at the level of individual experience of the body' (Watson *et al.* 1996: 170). Within the parameters of professional understanding, male embodiment remains largely 'unproblematic', fixed and immutable. In response, this book seeks to illuminate something of the nature of male embodiment and its relationship to health, culture and identity.

In exploring how ordinary men experience the body in everyday life, I would support the notion that one is, in fact, advocating a 'sociology of embodiment' rather than a 'sociology of the body' (Watson *et al.* 1996; Nettleton and Watson 1998a: 4). The former focuses on experience oscillating between structure and agency, the latter has been more concerned with theorizing the body. Arguably, it is the work of Merleau-Ponty (1962) and others working in the phenomenological or interpretative tradition (Young 1989; Leder 1992; Csordas 1994; Bendelow and Williams 1995; Crossley 1995) that has served to open up our appreciation of embodiment (to get at practical experience) and enabled us to move beyond some of the theoretical impasse that has bedevilled study of the body. Chapter 2 provides a more detailed critique of the state of 'sociology of the body' as the basis for this assertion. At this point, my purpose is simply to sketch out the terrain between 'the body' and 'embodiment'. Alexandra Howson (1996) provides a pithy tautology: the body = objectified, social other; embodiment = subjective experience of the body; embodied experience = the interaction between subjective and objective bodies. Taking this further, she says that embodiment refers to

> a dialectical process between embodied experience and the language available to articulate such experience. Hence, the notion of embodiment refers to a process of transformation and mediation in which embodied experience is authentic and articulated through cultural categories.
>
> (Howson 1998: 237)

One of these cultural categories is the lifecourse and, in part, this book looks to explore the issue of how embodiment and embodied experience might be affected by lifecourse transitions such as marriage and parenthood. In this context, the notion of the lifecourse warrants further consideration.

Embodiment and the lifecourse

Levinson (1978) has sought to demonstrate, from a social science perspective, that the lifecourse of the adult male is defined by passage through a number of discrete stages, such as early, middle and late adulthood. In anthropology, Van Gennep (1960) and Victor Turner (1969) have demonstrated that in traditional societies specific rituals and celebrations usually marked the passage from one stage to the next. By contrast, Featherstone and Hepworth (1991: 375) offer a more reflective 'take' on this structured and normative lifecourse, when they argue that

> Adult life . . . is a process . . . which need not involve predetermined series of stages of growth. The stages or hurdles . . . can be shifted around and even discarded. Yet, . . . we must be careful not to adopt a view of the lifecourse in which culture is granted the overarching power to mould nature in any form it chooses. Human beings share with other species an embodied existence inevitably involving birth, growth, maturation and death.

This view of an embodied lifecourse that encompasses both culture and biology leads us into the debates between modernists and postmodernists. These debates are important because they challenge basic assumptions about how we experience and make sense of the world around us. Modernism is located in the Enlightenment and presumes the existence of externally verifiable realities that can be uncovered through rational thought and scientific study. Levinson's notion of discrete stages in the development of the adult male fits within this view of the world. By contrast, postmodernists argue that social life is not an objective reality awaiting our attention; that society, organizations, communities, families and individuals do not exist beyond our subjective experience of them. That is, they are realized or constructed only through conversation, thought and writing. Giddens (1990) has mapped out the domain between modernism and postmodernism, arguing that there is not an easy distinction between the two. In essence, he appears to argue that postmodernism is a reflexive engine within modernism:

> The break with providential views of history [modernism], the dissolution of foundationalism, together with the emergence of counterfactual future-orientated thought and the 'emptying out' of progress by continual change, are so different from the core perspectives of the Enlightenment as to warrant the view that far-reaching transitions have occurred. Yet referring to these as post-modernity is a mistake which hampers an accurate understanding of their nature and implications. The disjunctions which have taken place should rather be seen as resulting from the self-clarification of modern thought, as the remnants of tradition and providential outlooks are cleared away. We have not moved beyond modernity but are living precisely through a phase of its radicalisation.
>
> (Giddens 1990: 51)

Elsewhere, in response to the postmodernist position, it has been suggested that cultural stereotypes of differing elements of the lifecourse remain important in deciding what is appropriate health behaviour. Adopting this position, Backett and Davison (1992: 56) argue that there are three ways of expressing such stereotypes: as cultural versions of physiological ageing; in terms of demographic status; and in terms of occupation. In this sense, the lifecourse of both men and women is overlain with a cultural patina reflected in and projected from the individual's body. As part of this process there are obvious distinctions between female and male bodies. Women experience menstruation, pregnancy, childbirth and the menopause. Existing literature would suggest that men do not experience these in an embodied sense, except in so far as the phenomenon of the couvade (Klein 1991; Csordas 1993) has been documented and that the existence of a male 'menopause' has been postulated. For women, menstruation, menopause and similar stages in the cycle of maturation are examples of stages in the female lifecourse wherein culture interprets and defines the biological (Martin 1989). Similarly, in Chapter 4 it will be suggested that lifecourse transitions for men are also marked by changes in embodied experience. However, this is not to posit a cultural determinism ascendant and in opposition to theories of biological determinism. In the context of embodied existence, this represents a false dichotomy. Rather, the concept of embodiment as the personal ground of culture (Csordas 1990) enmeshes nature and culture in an embodied existence. In this context it is the embodied human being who experiences a lifecourse socially structured by key life events such as starting school, getting a job, marriage, parenthood and bereavement.

Additionally, the embodied lifecourse is positioned and given meaning within structural circumstances other than gendered psychobiological and key life events. These include historical, cultural, scientific, economic and social circumstances. For the embodied individual, these interdependent biological, psychological and social processes are encapsulated in the personal narratives within which people create and sustain their sense of self and explain unfolding biographical experience (Berger and Luckman 1971; Kleinmann 1988; Davison *et al.* 1991). In sum, this book is centred on the notion that embodiment is the personal ground of culture, structure and behaviour and that focusing on embodied experience enables us to look at health in the context of these themes (Watson *et al.* 1996: 164). However, in putting embodiment into play one has to be mindful of the broader social and public health context that provides the terrain for embodied experience, an issue which is addressed in Chapter 1.

Embodiment and the problem of method

Method aside, there are different ways of 'getting at' embodiment. I fell into it by accident. 'The body' and 'embodiment' were categories that emerged during analysis of early interviews. They had not been present as I began fieldwork. By contrast, other colleagues working in Scotland on 'health in the middle years' and 'physical disability' began their work with a theoretical perspective regarding the potential salience of the body. Where all three studies came together was in their need to develop 'culturally acceptable and sensitive ways to ask about bodies' (Watson *et al.* 1996). A methodological challenge for a sociology of embodiment is to start addressing the need for conceptual tools that would enable the articulation of lay ideas about and experiences of the body that have previously been treated as inexpressible. Here, I am concerned with the ordinary, unexceptional bodies embedded in the detritus of daily living rather than bodies excavated by the drama, for example, of illness (Murphy 1987), screening (Howson 1998), care (Lawler 1991), or birth (Martin 1989).

Mindful of Frank's (1991) admonition that empirical enquiry should facilitate theoretical understanding, a grounded theory approach (Glaser and Strauss 1967; Glaser 1978; McCraken 1988) was used as a way of overcoming what can be identified as some of the limitations of current theorizing to deal with embodiment (see Chapter 3). In accessing lay accounts of embodiment it is not my intention to promote grounded theory as a universal method for getting at 'authentic' lay perspectives. As I have noted elsewhere (Nettleton and Watson 1998a: 20) there are diverse ways of getting at embodied experience. However, it provided a possible means of accessing the taken-for-granted status of embodiment and a means to move the analysis beyond description and into explanation. That is, analysis was concerned with explicating the processes and stages whereby the researcher moves from the 'discovery' of cultural (emic) categories to the application, testing and organization of analytical (etic) categories. Description alone is insufficient if one of the tasks of this research is to add to a body of knowledge capable of informing action to improve health. In particular, health promotion, as Kelly (1989) has put it, is a practical discipline whose essence lies in processes and as such requires more than description. However, this in its turn raises some interesting questions regarding the co-opting of lay knowledge into the quest to improve health (see Chapter 2).

Beyond description

Grounded theory has established procedures that, if followed, produce substantive theory or conceptual definitions of reality that are inherently valid, verifiable and applicable. In that sense, its strength is that these procedures can be documented and therefore some assessment made of the quality and fit between data, methods and findings. It is particularly useful in making sense of informant accounts that contain subjective phenomena that are best interpreted from the perspective of the informant. In a sense, it provides a means whereby lay knowledge can be excavated from everyday experience. It also provides an answer to the problem of how to move away from preconceptions with which the researcher enters the field since it frees the researcher 'to discover what is going on, rather than assuming what should be going on' (Glaser 1978: 159).

Grounded theory is characterized by an inductive–deductive process. The key to this process is theoretical sampling. The inductive element of grounded theory is based on the emergence of theory from data. The deductive process 'drives' this forward through the purposeful selection of samples or issues to 'check out' emerging theory. This process continues until the theory is sufficiently refined and its dimensions identified. Like Charmaz (1990) and Lützén and Nordin (1993), theoretical sampling occurred later than the initial sampling of people and places. It helped to shape later data collection, leading to the development of conceptual ideas rather than simply continuing to gather general data.

Three data sets were available to me in writing this book: a series of 90 in-depth unstructured and semi-structured interviews (60 fully transcribed and 30 note-coded) with a purposively selected sample of 30 men; field notes derived from immediate recollection of interviews; and field notes based on observations of well man clinics run at a local health centre.

The grounded theory approach to the collection, coding and analysis of data was used to illuminate three levels of analysis: first, the identification of cultural categories that gave meaning to informant beliefs regarding health, body and self-image and their interconnections; second, the development of analytical categories through identification of their general and abstract properties; and third, the organization of these categories and their dimensions into hierarchies with one or possibly two dominant explanatory concepts leading to the development and playing-out of substantive theory. Stern and Pyles (1986: 15) have argued that '[t]o be credible, the core variables, or theory, must be well integrated, easy to understand, relevant to the empirical world, and must explain the major variation in the process or phenomena studied'. However, I experienced two main problems with the analytical process described by Glaser and Strauss. First, it was not always possible, or desirable, to separate out cultural and analytical categories. A category may serve both as a cultural and an analytical category. In reality, the interpenetrating of categories moves both ways between cultural and analytical levels. For example, an informant's definition of being healthy may contain both clinical (height–weight ratios) and behavioural (eating, drinking, exercise) elements, together with some form of social as opposed to scientific explanation. Second, although it should, theoretically, be possible to organize one's analytical categories into hierarchical relationships, it may be inappropriate to 'force' categories into such a relationship where no obvious 'fit' occurs. In this instance, it may be more appropriate and theoretically justifiable to describe and explore the nature of the relationships between different categories.

There is another issue to consider in using grounded theory. That is the idea that if properly applied it 'frees' the researcher from *a priori* assumptions. Understanding is a social phenomenon – one of shared 'meanings'. Wax (1971: 13) has argued that understanding is acquired through socialization, implying that it emerges out of prolonged immersion in the culture being studied, that is to say, through participant observation. Since this option was not feasible, consideration had to be given to other means of ensuring that, as far as possible, the researcher was uncovering, recording and understanding the world-view(s) of the informants and not simply incorporating their accounts into his (the researcher's) own world-view or frame of reference.

A question of attribution

The issue of participant or respondent validation is one that has been discussed widely (Bloor 1978; McKeganey and Bloor 1981; MacPherson and Williamson 1992), but there is some disagreement about its value in research. Bloor (1978: 548–9) argues that respondent validation attempts to achieve a 'correspondence between sociologists' and members' views of the members' social world by exploring the extent to which members recognise, give assent to, the judgements of the sociologists'.

Participant validation is an essential part of the research process in qualitative research and should provide participants with the opportunity to make their own assessments of the validity of a researcher's findings (Bloor 1978). For example, data collection 'involves engaging in an active dialogue with research participants to check that we are understanding them as accurately as possible' (Secker *et al.* 1995: 77). Others would agree with such sentiments but caution that there are limits regarding the degree to which the researcher can, or should, incorporate informants' views into the written product of any research (Hammersley and Atkinson 1983: 196–7; MacPherson and Williamson 1992: 12). Hammersley and Atkinson (1983) comment that one should not assume that the informant provides a 'privileged' commentary upon his or her own actions, that is, that respondent accounts are especially truthful or complete. This issue of the validity of informant accounts is also addressed in the classic ethnographic literature (Turner 1960; Griaule 1975). Whilst acknowledging that respondent validation may have some shortcomings, I take the view that, on balance, validation can add to the research process. It does this by furnishing the researcher with different perspectives on the data that can widen the study beyond the 'limiting' theoretical baggage with which the researcher begins to gather data. It helps warn of any divergence of views between researcher and informant and uncover multiple perceptions of informants. Finally, it provides an 'indication of the extent or degree to which certain conditions or phenomena exist' (MacPherson and Williamson 1992: 10).

In short, participant validation provides a form of data and analytical triangulation.

The question that arose was how to fit informant validation into the research process. In this study, participant validation was part of the ongoing data collection, coding and fieldwork analysis stages of the research process. Key data in each phase of interviewing were validated through collection in subsequent interview phases. Preliminary analysis was undertaken to identify emerging themes and patterns during and after each phase of interviewing. This showed possible avenues of enquiry for the next research phase. The resultant research strategy was validated primarily to the extent to which lines of enquiry were able to generate additional data to build upon data collected about a particular emergent theme in a preceding interview phase. It was also confirmed by the degree to which informants 'recognized' the existence of certain conditions or phenomena and their relevance in the context of informant experience i.e. their representativeness.

The corpus of interview data is therefore analysed in and for itself. The data contains its own integrity and this is assessed by giving informants the opportunity to reflect back on what they have said. I have adopted the position of holding informant accounts to be data that 'display cultural realities which are neither biased nor accurate, but simply "real"' (Silverman 1985: 157). Of course, there may be a tendency to view the interview data, the narratives and stories contained within the transcripts, as less 'real' than data obtainable through quantitative means such as psychometric testing. However, to adopt this line of argument is to miss a crucial point – that informant accounts are real in so far as informants believe them to be real. That is, they have meaning, although informants may be selective in what they disclose to the researcher, and the core elements remain consistent, that is, they appear repeatedly in informant accounts. The importance of this perspective for data gathered through the ethnographic interview is stated by Mullen (1993: 33) when he says that 'language is a repository of cultural stocks of knowledge of the social world, and it is these stocks of knowledge that the ethnographic interview seeks to uncover'.

Grounded theory is particularly useful here because it works on the basis of identifying and verifying the consistency of categories and their properties through a procedure of constant comparison within and across data.

A further implication is the degree to which the construction of personal accounts, as such, influences the way in which informants make choices regarding lifestyles. Of course, this still leaves the issue of whether informants' beliefs are matched in their behaviour. In this research, the concern was with informants' beliefs regarding the relationship between self-image, body image and health. As part of this, one may be concerned with their perceptions of behaviour, but one is not concerned with verifying that the behaviour occurs.

In this study, I was also aware of another aspect of the status of the data. The aim of the series of interviews was to enable both the informant and the researcher to move beyond 'public' accounts of health and self to access more private and potentially sensitive health narratives. Here the researcher fills a privileged position. Particularly during the course of first- and third-round interviews, some informants commented that they 'don't talk about their health' with other men. The men in this study would not usually talk about 'health' with anyone other than their partner or general practitioner (and colleagues at work in certain instances – for example, joking about having 'the snip' and its side-effects) unless it was in the context of an interview. There are obvious ethical dilemmas implicit in this 'privileged' status – not least because it allows the idea that the researcher, by getting the informants to talk about health, something they do not normally do, has the potential for encouraging reflection about and alteration of existing practices related to health.

The participants

In anthropology, Geertz (1993) argues that the researcher can apply anthropological thinking to the study of modern thought and behaviour by looking to the 'natural communities' in our midst – groupings that share ways of perceiving, articulating and experiencing the world. Martin (1989) was interested in examining women's experience of menstruation, pregnancy, childbirth and menopause and took 'women' as her 'natural community'. Her sample was allowed to self-select on the basis that though the informants may have had access to or control over differing resources, roles and status, their experiences as women – partner, mother, worker, carer – derived from culturally approved and mediated stereotypes. The only overt criteria employed by Martin in sample selection was that it reflected the composition of the reference population in Baltimore in terms of ethnic, social and age distributions. In this particular instance, mirroring the heterogeneity of the population justified the generalizability of the findings. At the other end of the scale, Backett (1990, 1992a, 1992b), in her study of health in middle-class families, worked with a small homogeneous sample of 28 families. Her sampling criteria promoted homogeneity, and followed the process of theoretical sampling advocated by Glaser and Strauss (1967).

The particular community in which this study was based lies to the south of Aberdeen in North East Scotland. Originally, it was a typical North East fishing village, but with the first North Sea oil boom in the early 1970s the area was zoned for a massive expansion of housing to meet demand for accommodation for people working directly in or supporting the oil industry. Housing growth slowed with the slump in oil production in the 1980s but picked up again during the early 1990s. About one-tenth of the housing stock is local authority housing. The community has a high proportion of young families and is served by a health centre, two primary schools and a high school. Next to the high school is a modern swimming pool complex, but there are no other leisure facilities. On the northern side the community is bounded by several light industrial units generally servicing the offshore oil industry, a slaughterhouse, a purpose-built retail site and the main road route between Aberdeen and the south. On the southern side the new housing stock is bounded by the main East Coast railway line, which also provides a boundary between most of the original village and the newer housing. A few smaller shops are scattered across the community.

Within this community the study focused upon men in the 30–40 age group because there was little evidence that the health beliefs of this male age group had been explored (the original purpose of the study). Those men who took part in the study were similar not only in terms of age and role but also in the sharing of 'middle-class' consumer values, leading to the construction of similar lifestyles (see Bourdieu 1984; Featherstone 1991).[2] About half came from what they described as working-class backgrounds in Glasgow, the North of England, Aberdeen and its rural hinterland, and crofting communities in the North of Scotland. However, lifestyle is not simply about patterns of consumption or behaviour shaped by prevailing social and economic circumstances. It is also informed, for some of the men who took part, by the social values learnt in childhood in these communities, such as the role of the father and the family and the importance of work.[3]

Another way of looking at this process of moving into the social world of the adult male is to see it as a process of 'fitting in'. Some informants tended to the view that as you get older, work, family and friends broaden your horizons. You start to mix with other people who may hold different attitudes and display different lifestyles. In turn you get involved in a process of 'picking up' and discarding 'bits and pieces' from your own and their lifestyles. One informant, who describes himself as coming from a very poor working-class background and whose work as a car salesman requires a degree of ability in determining and 'mirroring' his customer's lifestyle and aspirations, commented:

> To mix with them socially you have to adopt their lifestyle as well, or not adopt it and try to find other people as interesting from different social backgrounds or with different interests in life. . . . I don't think there are social classes, but there are certain aspects of behaviour that you find acceptable and interesting . . . It's like me being in the company of the Duke and Duchess of York. We have absolutely nothing in common. We are as different as chalk and cheese. I wouldn't know what to say to them and vice versa. Whereas if you put me in a normal working-class background, they have the same upbringing as I have so

I feel comfortable. I don't necessarily agree with the way they actually lead their social life . . . but if I want to meet with people of the same social structure I have then got to adopt to a certain extent their social styles.

(Car salesman, 36)

This informant is making a crucial point. Although he lives in what could be described as a middle-class neighbourhood with aspirations to a particular lifestyle, to 'fit in' his account shows that a person can claim that their relatedness to others is not necessarily governed by the values and attitudes that guide choices regarding consumption and lifestyle.

At the time when I initially entered the lives of the men who took part in the research, 27 were married, two had remarried following divorce and one informant was in a common-law marriage. By the end of the study, two of those who were married had separated from their partners. Thirteen informants had left school by the time they were 16 while four had gone on to complete an apprenticeship. Of the remainder one had left school at age 18 with A levels, seven had gone on to further education to obtain Ordinary or Higher National Diplomas, four were graduates and one a postgraduate.

In terms of housing tenure, most of the informants were owner/occupiers (24), and the rest rented from the local council (4) or from their current employer (2). In the area of the study, a large number of men work either directly or indirectly in the North Sea oil industry. Of those recruited, one informant was in a manual oil-related job and four were in non-oil-related manual jobs. Thirteen men were in non-manual oil-related jobs and 11 worked in non-manual jobs outwith that sector. One informant was unemployed.

The men who took part in the study were not necessarily health conscious. Of the 30, ten were cigarette smokers initially (though two gave up during the course of the study), four were ex-cigarette smokers, one was an ex-cigarette smoker who now smoked cigars and the rest had never smoked cigarettes or had only experimented when young. All the informants drank alcohol, but there was no evidence that any of the informants drank above the recommended safe drinking levels of 21 units a week for men (Royal College of General Practitioners 1986: 30–2; Royal College of Psychiatrists 1986: 178), although many had done so before marriage. Only seven of the informants took regular exercise.

In considering the potential generalizability of the findings presented in the following chapters, it needs to be emphasized that in communities in North East Scotland, such as the one in which the informants lived, employment and incomes are generally higher than elsewhere in Scotland. This is largely due to the jobs and wages available for working in the offshore oil industry and related sectors for both manual and non-manual workers.

This has led to increased social mobility and material resources for those men attracted to the area. So, although some informants come from 'working-class' backgrounds it would be difficult to claim that they are representative of males in this age cohort who live in areas of high unemployment. It is evident, for example, that most informants now have money, expectations and social circumstances that are very different from some of the areas which they grew up in.

A final word on the use of quotations

To avoid altering informants' meanings or imposing researcher-grounded meanings, informants are quoted verbatim. Researcher interjections, long pauses and repetitive speech mannerisms have been left out. Where this is done it is indicated by means of ellipsis (. . .). Quotation marks indicate where other words, phrases or short sentences have been incorporated into the text. Informants' names and pseudonyms are not used to label the quotations. Usage of these adds nothing to our knowledge of the informant and probably speaks volumes about the lack of imagination of the researcher. The convention adopted in labelling quotations and longer accounts in the following chapters will be to use the informant's age and a slightly modified occupation type.

Notes

1 Sabo and Gordon (1995) provide a useful example of the application of this analytical distinction between the personal and the social.
2 The minimum sample size sought for this study was 25 informants. It was intended that potential informants be randomly selected from the practice register of a local health centre using the Community Health Index (CHI). At the time of sampling (June 1991) over 1000 men in the 30–40 age group were registered with the practice. It was decided that 100 men aged 30–40, married and registered with the practice, be randomly sampled from the CHI following clearance from the general medical practitioner (GP) responsible for running the well man clinic. The GP agreed to facilitate these aspects of the study following a meeting at which the aims and focus of the study and the study design were explained.

Based on previous experience of responses to studies using similar methods of 'cold' recruitment, it was anticipated that around one-third of those contacted might agree to participate. It was intended that those men who had been randomly sampled be sent a letter from the health centre, letting them know that a study into 'men's health' was to take place locally. The letter indicated that the study had the support of the practice and asked them if they were willing to be considered for participation in the study. If they were interested they were instructed to tear off a response slip and return it to the practice manager.

Alternative sampling approaches were considered, for example the 'snowball technique' whereby one or two initial informants are recruited and then recommend other potential informants to the researcher. Another approach considered was that used by Williams (1990) who recruited his informants from established working- and middle-class networks in Aberdeen. The chosen approach was adopted since it was not essential that the informants knew each other, simply that they shared some of the same life situations. It was also felt that this would make the findings of the study more generalizable to men in this lifecourse category than if the informants had come from a particular shared situation. Like the women in Martin's (1989) study, it was assumed that the men in this study would share ways of perceiving the world (see also Geertz's notion of 'natural communities').

Whilst most informants responded as described, a few telephoned the practice manager instead. Of the 100 men randomly sampled from the CHI by one of the CHI information officers, 23 responded at this stage and were approached through a telephone call from the researcher. Of these 23, 19 met the recruitment criteria and were recruited to the study. Criteria for recruitment were that informants should not have attended a well man clinic in the preceding three years and should be in a stable relationship and have children either with a past or current partner. Focusing on men who were or had been married, or were otherwise in a stable relationship, and had children, was felt important in order to explore the issue of how embodiment might be affected by lifecourse transitions such as marriage and parenthood. Those who did not meet the criteria were sent a letter thanking them for their response. Since the minimum sample size sought for this study was 25 it was decided to seek a further random sample from the CHI, and a further 100 men were randomly sampled. The same recruitment procedure was followed and a further 11 men were eventually recruited, bringing the total number of informants to 30. Of the 30 men recruited at the start of the study, nine were aged 30–33, nine 34–37 and twelve 38–40.

3 Williams (1990) provides a clear and thoughtful account of health-related social values among an older generation of Aberdonians.

CHAPTER 1

DOMINANT PERSPECTIVES SHAPING MEN'S HEALTH

Men's health has increasingly exercised the attention of the media during the 1990s. Reports of increasing stress, declining fertility, Viagra, rising obesity, prostate and testicular cancer, ignorance of our bodies and a marked reluctance to visit the doctor – all have fuelled the growing debate about the state of men's health and what to do about it. Recent health statistics for the UK paint a depressing picture. They show that women live five years longer than men. The figures also reveal that the overall death rate from accidents and violence is almost double for men compared to women and that the difference is even higher for road traffic accidents and suicides in the 15–34 age group. By contrast, in later life more men die from heart disease and lung cancer.

A prevailing explanation for such differences, among health professionals, is that poor men's health results from their trying to live up to a macho image and that male lifestyles are dangerous to health. In this respect it is suggested that men and women face different risks based on biology, sex roles, stress, lifestyles and preventive health practices. Thus, the life expectancy of a baby boy born in Scotland in 1997 was 72.6 years, one of the lowest in the Western world; this is thought to be caused by a mixture of lifestyle, genetic and physiological factors such as the protective effects of oestrogen in pre-menopausal women. Also important are psychosocial factors such as how men and women evaluate symptoms and their willingness to take some therapeutic action.

It has been said that macho attitudes and health do not mix and that, in a health sense, men are the 'weaker' sex (Sabo and Gordon 1995). In truth, the research that has addressed the impact of masculinity on health is as confused as our ideas of what it is 'to be a man'. For example, researchers who have analysed findings from a major ongoing study of the social patterning of health in the west of Scotland (Annandale and Hunt 1990) have concluded that masculine traits in both men and women could be implicated in more positive health outcomes. Yet other research would suggest that because men are reluctant to go to the doctor for 'minor' complaints, this hides a lot of day-to-day illness and injury not recorded officially (Verbrugge 1985, 1989). There is a view that men do not like to go public on minor things but will suffer in silence or rely on their partners for sympathy (Good et al. 1989). It certainly seems to be that men do not demand services and are reluctant to use those that are available to them. Paradoxically, a popular view among many women is that, '[t]o the average man, a bad cold has five-act potential and he will use it to extract every last drop of sympathy' (Bradford 1995).

Changing policy agendas

In the early 1990s public health policy statements such as *The Health of the Nation* (Department of Health (DoH) 1992) and *Scotland's Health: A Challenge to Us All* (Scottish Office Department of Health (SODoH) 1992) stressed the importance of individual health behaviours and lifestyles in determining health outcomes. Such statements were based on two assumptions: that an individual can influence personal decisions regarding lifestyle; and that changes in lifestyle can, in turn, significantly affect health outcomes. In this respect, much attention has been paid to the development and application of theories (Rogers and Shoemaker 1971; Bem 1972; Ajzen and Fishbein 1977; Bandura 1977; Wallston et al. 1978) and models (Becker 1974; Tones 1987) of health behaviour. For example, the 'health action model' (Tones 1987) incorporates several other theories and models which have contributed towards health promotion practice and which principally focus on the processes of psychological change.

However, concerns to invoke individual responsibility for health in national health policy statements in the early 1990s, whilst having ideological underpinnings, also coincided with global concerns about containing the escalating costs of health care. Certainly the (albeit imperfect) data on the cost-effectiveness, for example, of prevention of coronary heart disease (CHD) established a *prima facie* case for the targeting of scarce resources towards primary prevention, including screening and health education (SODoH, PHPU 1996).

This approach was and continues to be informed by a large literature suggesting that adverse early life experience, poor diet, cigarette smoking, high blood pressure, physical inactivity, raised total cholesterol and excessive alcohol consumption are implicated in the aetiology of cardiovascular and respiratory disease, some cancers and other conditions (DoH 1993; Lloyd 1996; SODoH 1996). Many of these risk factors are interrelated. To take excessive alcohol consumption as an example:

Misuse of alcohol is an established risk factor for a number of cancers; is commonly implicated in the causation of accidents; may affect sexual behaviour in such a way as to increase the risk of transmission of HIV and other [sexually transmitted diseases] and unwanted pregnancies; contributes to a number of dental/oral health problems including oral cancer and traumatic damage (through accidents and assaults); as a behaviour has links to use of tobacco and other drugs; is a risk factor for hypertension, which is in turn associated with CHD.

(Tannahill 1994: 4)

Further, a number of reports have demonstrated the higher prevalence of unhealthy behaviours such as smoking, alcohol consumption and poorer nutrition among men (DoH 1993; Dong and Erens 1997). In relation to CHD, Lloyd (1996: 16) has noted that:

While debate continues about what risk factors there are, who is at risk, and whether concentration on these factors impacts on mortality rates, the literature seems to travel parallel with the aspects of CHD that are about men's behaviour, beliefs and attitudes.

Unfortunately, the underpinning analysis fails to acknowledge that there are other factors that limit an individual's capacity for choice (Abel 1998). Thus, health risks become self-imposed when behaviour is not modified. As Lupton (1993: 432–3) has observed:

Health education emphasising risks is a form of pedagogy, which, like other forms, serves to legitimate ideologies and social practices. Risk discourse in the public health sphere allows the state, as the owner of knowledge, to exert power over the bodies of its citizens. Risk discourse, therefore, especially when it emphasises lifestyle risks, serves as an effective . . . agent of surveillance and control that is difficult to challenge because of its manifest benevolent goal of maintaining standards of health.

Viewed in this way, health education can be seen as a form of governance whereby society seeks to impose control on individuals through the promotion of specific forms of health behaviour aimed at controlling bodies. This informs what Tones has termed the traditional approach to health education. In this, the 'goal is to *persuade* the individual to adopt a particular lifestyle so as to prevent disease and thus reduce mortality and morbidity in the population', an approach which sits comfortably with the goals of orthodox preventive medicine (Tones 1986: 7).

By contrast, at an academic and at a practice level, health promotion has emerged as a reaction against traditional Western biomedical explanations for health and illness. Health promotion has been defined as 'the process of enabling people to increase control over, and to improve, their health' (World Health Organization (WHO) 1986). This 'hybrid activity' (Naidoo and Daykin 1995) is grounded in a sociostructural paradigm as opposed to a biomedical paradigm. Sociostructural theories are underpinned by a critique that argues that individual behaviour and lifestyle choices are inevitably constrained by structural factors such as occupation, gender, race and housing. Thus, a new emphasis is placed upon the facilitation of healthy lives by altering the social, economic and ecological environments within which people live (Bunton *et al.* 1995). This is reflected in a recent health promotion glossary which defines the process of health promotion as one that embraces actions directed at strengthening the skills and capabilities of people and also those directed towards changing social, environmental and economic conditions which create and sustain health (Nutbeam 1998).

Bridging these two paradigms one finds proponents of a socioecological framework for theories related to health promotion (Anon. 1992). This framework is based on the assumption that 'critical improvements in the environment and lifestyle could lead to a significant reduction in morbidity and mortality' (WHO 1986). Underpinning this development has been an implicit notion that health and illness are

> not simply matters concerning human bodies and their functions. Rather these states and the transition between them represent a complex inter-play of physiological conditions, the cultural structures of which give them meaning, and the social organisations and interactions within which they are situated.
>
> (Backett and Davison 1995: 629)

In part, this has been propelled by a recognition of the constructed and contingent nature of medical knowledge and thus a rejection of the determinacy of biological explanations of social and cultural phenomena as they relate to individuals' experiences of health and illness. Thus, as noted by Backett (1989: 141), 'health related behaviours should be studied not simply as individually determined but rather as social products which are subject to complex structural and interactional constraints'. In the sociology of health and illness this has led to a particular focus, not only on lay concepts of health and illness, but especially on the everyday contexts of health-related behaviour (Cornwall 1984; Backett 1992a and 1992b; Backett and Davison 1992; Mullen 1993).

The call for a greater explicit recognition of the importance of context for behaviour has been seen as one way of engaging in a more construct- ive partnership with lay groups, especially those who are marginalized and disadvantaged (Rogers *et al.* 1997: 34; Abel 1998). Arguably, men can be counted as one of those groups (Variations Sub-Group of the Chief Medical Officers Health of the Nation Working Group 1996). Similarly, Macintyre (1997: 740) warns of the importance of social context, saying that it 'needs continually to be taken into account and is likely to result in and require more differentiated and sophisticated explanatory models of social health inequalities'. Thus, to be effective, public health and health promotion need to be sensitive to the ways in which structure (and behav- iour) is experienced in the everyday lifeworlds of individuals. Elsewhere, Popay *et al.* (1998) argue that current theories and research on inequalities in health are limited because they do not adequately address the relationship between agency and structure and the role of lay knowledge in this respect (this argument is examined in more detail in Chapter 3). Perhaps some- what self-critically, this chapter presages an argument developed through the remainder of the book that, in public health and health promotion, our understanding of the individual is currently inadequately problematized. This not only has implications for the expectations we harbour regarding the efficacy of interventions targeting the individual, but also is important in considering the interrelationship of human agency and action to improve health at the community, organizational and structural levels.

Nevertheless, the publication of New Labour's consultation policy papers on improving health – *Our Healthier Nation* (DoH 1998) and *Working Together for a Healthier Scotland* (SODoH, 1998b) – has marked a signific- ant shift in health policy. In a sense, the desire to address the social and economic determinants of health – alongside a continuing commitment to influence lifestyles – can be characterized as a desire to maintain and enhance health at all levels of society, albeit within an implicit values framework (Downie *et al.* 1993; Tannahill 1998). This raises an important point, often glossed over. Though the recognition of social context is critical and to be welcomed, it can act to obscure a more fundamental tension between pub- lic and personal moralities in *late modernity*. Whatever one's 'take' on the relative importance of agency and structure in the paradigms outlined above, they are in turn emblematic of a public health enterprise unerringly driven by a moral imperative (Lupton 1995). This moral imperative is concerned with regulating the bodies of individuals and populations through tech- niques of surveillance (Armstrong 1995; see also Armstrong 1983 on epi- demiology and general practice; Nettleton 1988 on dentistry) and promotion of technologies of the self (Foucault 1988; Petersen 1997). In this respect, the body has become a site for control and change through lifestyle dir- ectives in recent years (Crawford, 1984; Beattie 1991; Bunton 1992). This reflects theoretical treatment of 'the body' as a vehicle for social control (see particularly Foucault 1973, 1979; Arney and Neill 1982; Douglas 1982; Turner 1984; Nettleton 1988).

Arguably, such developments in the policy agenda can be seen as opening up new opportunities for surveillance (Armstrong 1983, 1995). This perspective is informed by Foucault's (1973, 1979) work which gave an impetus to the identification and examination of new forms of governance and concomitant techniques of surveillance. The extension of these strategies to encompass the economic and social circumstances in which people live can perhaps be viewed as a reflexive systems response to uncertainty – particularly, a desire to manage the human consequences engendered by the broad social transformations of globalization, the advent of new cyber- and information technologies, the changing nature of the disease burden, ageing populations and the rise of consumer culture (Featherstone 1991; Giddens 1991; Beck 1992; Featherstone and Burrows 1995).

The epidemiological picture

Generally, I would argue that in the context of the broad social transformations under way in developed countries our approach to gender and health requires a more sensitive reading of the impact of macro socioeconomic trends that is exacerbating, among some social groups, a long-established male disadvantage in health. A female over male advantage in life expectancy

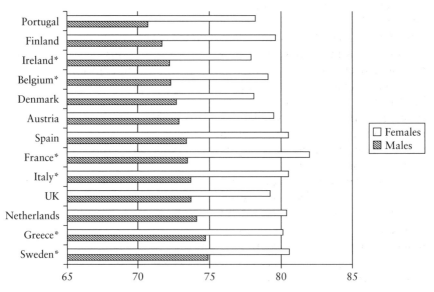

Figure 1.1 Life expectancy at birth by sex and country, 1992
Source: WHO (1994)
*1992 data not available

emerged in the latter part of the nineteenth century (Hart 1988), although some contemporary research suggests that, in some countries this differential was already well established.[1] Findings from Australia (Van Buynder and Smith 1995), Sweden (Ekenstam 1998), the United States (Verbrugge 1985, 1989) and United Kingdom (Lloyd 1996) demonstrate a consistent pattern of male disadvantage in terms of life expectancy (see Figure 1.1),[2] excess mortality across all age groups and an increasing gap between men and women in terms of risk behaviours associated with cardiovascular disease, although there is a greater use of hospitals by women. However, life expectancy cannot be taken in isolation. For example, in the Netherlands Ruwaard and Kramers (1998) distinguish between life expectancy and 'health expectancy'. Although measurement of the former shows that Dutch women can still expect to live longer than men, both sexes enjoy about 60 years of 'good health'. They found that during the period 1983–94, improvement in the life expectancy of men was attended by a slight increase in the number of 'healthy' years for men and a slight decline for women (Ruwaard and Kramers 1998: 42–6).

Mortality

Since the beginning of the twentieth century, mortality rates have fallen and life expectancy has increased significantly throughout the developed world. However, Figure 1.2 illustrates the higher mortality rates seen in men at all ages in Scotland over the past 20 years. The relative excess in male mortality is greatest in young adults, due largely to higher death rates from accidents and suicides. Among young adults, the excess mortality in men rose between 1975 and 1995 and the peak is broader – with substantially higher mortality among men than women between the ages of 15 and 29 years.

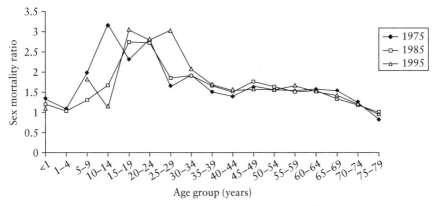

Figure 1.2 Sex mortality ratio, all causes, Scotland, 1975–95
Source: General Registrar Office for Scotland

Table 1.1 Death rates per 100,000, Scotland, 1997

Sex	External causes	Cancer	Diseases of the heart and circulation	Other
Ages 1–44				
Males	47	11	14	39
Females	14	16	7	19
Ages 45–64				
Males	62	339	410	229
Females	26	273	171	150

Source: Scottish Office Department of Health (1998a)

This change is attributable in part to increases in deaths from suicide, drugs and AIDS.[3]

This pattern can be seen in more detail in Table 1.1. Explaining these figures, the Chief Medical Officer for Scotland's report notes that 'only 4% of deaths (2,593) occurred between the ages of 1 and 44 in 1997, a mortality rate of 0.8 per 1000'. The mortality rate for men was twice as high (1.0 per 1000) as for women (0.5). The major causes of death in this group were accidents, poisonings and violence for men and cancers for women. By contrast, 16% of deaths occurred in the 45–64 age group. The death rate for men was 9.8 per 1000 compared to 5.8 for women. Diseases of the circulatory system contributed 40% of deaths in men, mostly from ischaemic heart disease (294 per 100,000). The mortality rate for stroke was 53 per 100,000. Among women the rates were 90 and 39 per 100,000 respectively (SODoH 1998a: 39).

Whilst the above data are indicative of a general male health disadvantage, an analysis by Drever and Bunting (1997) of patterns and trends in male mortality in England and Wales between 1991 and 1993 clearly demonstrates a social class gradient in all-cause mortality and a widening social class differential for stroke, lung cancer, accidents and suicide over time. The standardized mortality ratio (SMR) by social class for men aged 20–64, for deaths from all causes, ranges from 66 in social class I to 189 (almost three times as high) in social class V (Drever and Bunting 1997: 97).

Figure 1.3 shows age-specific mortality rates for men aged 20–44. This clearly shows that social class I has the lowest mortality rate at each age. Classes II and I have similar rates from age 40. The difference across the classes is even more marked in these younger age groups than in those aged 45–64. Between 30 and 34, the death rate in class I is about one death per 700 men; in class V it is over four times this rate, at one death per 150 men.[4]

Trends in mortality in men aged 15–44 have been the subject of particular scrutiny because they have not mirrored the general fall in mortality

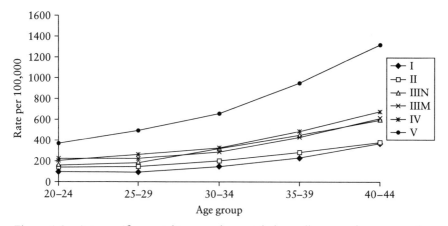

Figure 1.3   Age-specific mortality rates by social class, all causes, for men aged 20–44, England and Wales, 1991–93

Source: Drever and Bunting (1997). Reproduced by permission: 'Health Inequalities'. Office for National Statistics. ©Crown copyright 1998

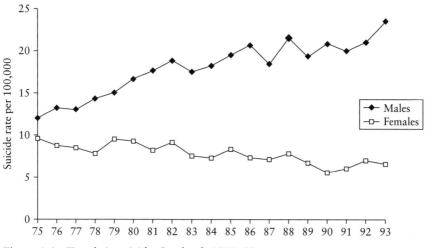

Figure 1.4   Trends in suicide, Scotland, 1975–93
Source: General Registrar Office for Scotland

seen in other age groups, even after demographic changes are taken into account. Mortality increased by 9% between 1981 and 1992 for men aged 15–44 living in deprived areas of Glasgow (McCarron *et al.* 1994: 1481). Deaths from AIDS, suicide and related to alcohol and drugs have all risen in this age group in the last ten years (DoH 1993: 85). Figure 1.4 shows the trends in suicide in Scotland among males and females aged 15+ for the period 1975–93.

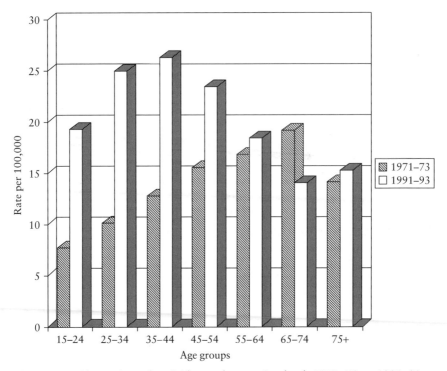

Figure 1.5 Change in male suicide rate by age, Scotland, 1971–73 to 1991–93
Source: General Registrar Office for Scotland

The striking divergence in trends between males and females masks a fundamental shift in the sociodemographic patterning of suicide among men. Figure 1.5 illustrates the nature of this shift by comparing changes in suicide rate by age in Scotland between 1971–73 and 1991–93. In 1971–73, there is a clear gradient in suicide rate from age 15–24 to ages 65–74, peaking at 19.2 per 100,000 in the latter age group. By contrast, in 1991–93 the suicide rate was highest in the 35–44 age group (at 26.3 per 100,000), an increase of 105% in that age group in the 20 years from 1971–73. More startling was the increase in suicides in the 15–24 age group (from 7.8 to 19.4, an increase of 149%) and the 25–34 age group (from 10.2 to 25.0, an increase of 145%).[5] Whilst suicide rates in Scotland rose across all deprivation categories, the increase was sharpest among young men living in deprived areas (McLoone 1996: 543).

It is difficult to attribute this shift to any one factor.[6] It has been suggested by Wilkinson (1997: 594) that 'socio-economic differences in mortality are at their maximum [between the ages of 20 and 40 for men] and the national trends are likely to be partly a reflection of the increased burden of relative deprivation'. McLoone and Boddy (1994) found that postcode sectors in

Scotland that were categorized as deprived in the 1981 Census were relatively more deprived by the time of the 1991 Census. More specifically, there were increases in the death rate for men (29%) and women (11%) aged 20–29 in deprived groups largely as a result of increases in suicide rates (McLoone and Boddy 1994: 1466). Relatedly, findings from research on unemployment show how it affects mortality (Carstairs and Morris 1991: 220–2) and psychosocial health (Platt 1984; Eales 1989). Taken together, it seems likely that the interaction of psychosocial health and changes in life circumstances (inadequate housing, not having a job, increased risk of crime – as victim or offender) and life chances (poorer educational attainment, being in low-paid or insecure work) for those marginalized by socioeconomic changes during the 1980s has had a disproportionate effect on younger men in social class V.

Morbidity

Mortality data alone are insufficient as a reliable indicator of men's health. As the Chief Medical Officer has observed (DoH 1993), health problems can be identified through an examination of morbidity data from various sources of information, though there is no consensus on what the key indicators might be. One indicator of serious health problems is discharges from hospital (see Table 1.2). Among men aged 15–44 in Scotland in 1997, there was a high rate of injury and poisonings, followed by digestive, musculoskeletal and respiratory problems. In the 45–64 age group

Table 1.2 Discharges from hospital per 100,000 population by principal diagnosis, Scotland, 1997

	Age	
Main diagnosis	*15–44*	*45–64*
Heart disease	283	3920
Stroke	35	409
Other	284	1123
Digestive system	2002	3976
Malignant neoplasms	521	3533
Signs, symptoms	1161	3074
Musculoskeletal	899	1429
Injury and poisoning	2670	1786
Respiratory diseases	700	1245
Mental disorders	171	278

Source: SMR1 Information and Statistics Division Scotland, Hospital Community Information

diseases of the circulatory and digestive systems and cancers became more important.

In Scotland, as in many other countries, social class differences in cardio-vascular disease morbidity and mortality have been reported, with socio-economically disadvantaged groups having higher risk (Pocock *et al.* 1987; Drever *et al.* 1996). Looking at prevalence of any cardiovascular disorder (angina, heart attack, stroke, hypertension, heart murmur, abnormal heart rhythm, diabetes and other heart trouble) the Scottish Health Survey 1995 found variations in the prevalence of any cardiovascular disorder between social classes. Prevalence was higher among those in the manual than in the non-manual classes, although no clear social gradient was seen in either sex. Among men, the age-standardized prevalence was lowest (12.4%) in the professional group (social class I) and highest in classes IIIM (19.5%) and V (19.4%) (Dong *et al.* 1997).

Another common morbidity indicator is general practitioner consulta-tions, given that the first point of contact with the National Health Service for most people in the UK is their GP. Although the proportion of both males and females consulting a GP has increased since 1971, it has increased at a faster rate among females. Women are also more likely to consult a GP than men. In 1996–97 the proportion was 19% for females and 13% for males (Office for National Statistics 1998). Findings from the Scottish Health Survey 1995 reveal that in Scotland, the proportion was 22% for females and 14% for males (Dong and Erens 1997).

GP consultation statistics (Table 1.3) reveal a broadly similar pattern in the older age group (consultations for cancers excepted and the import-ance of mental disorders and musculoskeletal conditions increasing) to that shown by hospital morbidity data. In the younger age group, mental, musculoskeletal and respiratory systems disorders are the primary reasons for consulting a GP. Further investigation would be needed, but it could be that injury and poisonings are mainly dealt with through accident and emergency departments. Given the strong association between high General Health Questionnaire (GHQ) score and employment status found in the 1995 Scottish Health Survey, particularly among unskilled workers (Dong and Erens 1997), the finding for mental disorders may not seem surprising. However, men, and younger men especially, seem less inclined to seek help for such problems. Self-reported health trends from the General Household Survey show that younger men reported fewer consultations with a GP in the previous year (Office for National Statistics 1995).

Recent analysis of reported consultation behaviour for 33 specified com-mon symptoms showed that women are significantly more likely to have consulted their GP for at least one symptom. However, the fact that more women reported experiencing more symptoms overall (including psycho-social symptoms) than men largely explained the differences in consultation rates (Wyke *et al.* 1998). Similarly, an analysis of GP consultations for

Table 1.3   GP consultation rates per 1000 males, Scotland, 1997

Disease/condition	Age 25–44	45–64
All diseases and conditions	1796.7	2679.4
Infectious and parasitic	77.3	66.2
Neoplasms	20.5	55.5
Endocrine/metabolic	27.3	107.9
Blood	3.1	6.6
Mental	265.1	260.1
Nervous system	103.6	150.8
Circulatory system	44.5	348.0
Respiratory system	252.8	334.8
Digestive system	96.7	132.4
Genitourinary system	29.3	47.2
Skin	125.4	137.6
Musculoskeletal	265.0	444.3
Symptoms, signs	148.1	238.3
Injury and poisonings	119.7	104.7
Others	387.2	590.6

Source: Information and Statistics Division Scotland, Continuous Morbidity Recording (CMR) Data

the most common chronic conditions reported in early and late mid-life showed that women are no more likely to consult than men, at a given level of reported severity for a given condition type, except in the case of mental health problems. In this respect, the authors comment that '[g]ender differences for mental health are probably greater than for other aspects of morbidity, and the aetiology of mental health problems may be more gender-specific than for other conditions' (Hunt *et al.* 1999: 99). Elsewhere, Munley and McGloughlin (1998) have explored gender differences in intention to attend health checks and related health beliefs among a sample of 60 men and 60 women in Manchester. Analysis showed that the women in their sample made more use of general health checks and had stronger intentions to use them in the future. This finding was underpinned by their finding that men and women have different health beliefs in relation to attending health checks.

   In general, the literature on men's health is dominated by epidemiological data and related research into the biological (and sexual) aspects of men's health and a related literature on risk (Lloyd 1996). The literature that takes masculinity and its impact on health as a starting point is mainly from the USA. In the UK context, masculinity is often seen 'as an inadequate model as men are not a homogeneous group' and because of a pragmatic view that if we target those who take risks, then men will be reached (Lloyd 1996: 6). This is a specious argument, in part because it views 'men' through an external prism of risk rather than attempting the more complex task of understanding how different groups of men perceive and grapple with the world around them. The literature on risk is an example of a dominant discourse in public health reflecting the fact that risk is perceived as a key feature that permeates modern society. Scientific knowledge is constructed around risk and the expertise required to manage risk (Giddens 1991; Beck 1992; Petersen 1997). However, as Lupton (1995: 80) notes: 'The risks which are selected by a society as requiring attention may . . . have no relation to "real" danger but are culturally identified as important'. Critically, as Lupton (1995: 81) goes on to assert, 'the notion of internally imposed risk has yet to be fully critiqued for its political and moral dimension', and it is this perception of risk, derived from clinical medicine and epidemiology, which informs health promotion.

Gender and health

I have suggested that action to improve health could be undermined by a failure adequately to understand and problematize male experience. Risk discourse constructs the individual, and especially the male, in a curiously lopsided way which, in its privileging of health above other agendas, is dissociated from more immediate everyday experience. That is, personal practice comes about in a changing structure of relationships, and gender is a way in which social practice is ordered (Connell 1995: 71–86). In this respect, the linked concepts of masculinity and practice are important since the challenge for practitioners and policy-makers is both to recognize and to respond to individual practice, 'where structural and everyday constraints interacting with social values shape and are shaped by the human experience of health, its maintenance and its loss' (Watson *et al.* 1996: 171). It is against this backdrop that my objective is now to explore contemporary thinking about the nature of masculinity and its contribution to understanding men's involvement in a gendered world, in particular the practical construction of masculinity in everyday life.

Gender and health: a woman's affair?

In 1998 the World Health Report included a spotlight on gender. This states that

> WHO, in applying a gender approach to health, moves beyond describing women and women's health in isolation, bringing into the analysis differences between women and men. It examines how these differences

determine differential exposure to risk, access to the benefits of technology and health care, rights and responsibilities, and the control of
people over their lives.

(WHO 1998a: 95)

In practice, the report continues, a gender approach leads to consideration
of the following points: factors that affect women's health; women's roles;
men's roles, perspectives and beliefs in relation to women's health concerns; women's participation in identifying health issues; lifetime experience
of women (WHO 1998a: 96).

In the context of development the gender and health argument is often
seen as synonymous with women and health. The comments from WHO
(1998a) are made in a global context and are important in that respect.
Relatedly, the Women's Health and Development Programme has published an elegant review of issues around gender and health (WHO 1998b).
The report marks a shift from an approach characterized as 'women in
development' to 'gender and development'. The former approach focused
on improving the access of women to services, education, credit facilities
and other resources. The latter approach is marked by an emphasis on gender equity and empowerment of women as the basis for planning effective
health and population programmes. Though this report recognizes that men's
health may be undermined by the 'ways in which gender roles are currently
constructed' (WHO 1998b: 11), the use of gender, in a global context, is
primarily articulated around an analysis of inequalities that arise from the
different roles of women and men, or the unequal power relations between
them and the consequences of this inequality on their lives and for health.

The interacting nature of factors, including gender, which contribute to
health inequalities was recognized by the Variations Sub-Group of the Chief
Medical Officer's Health of the Nation Working Group[7] in their report
Variations in Health (1996). The report opens with the statement that:

for several years now it has been well documented that across the
developed world, there are variations in the extent of sickness and
premature death between different groups within populations . . . These
variations . . . are associated with a range of often interacting factors:
geography, socio-economic status, gender, environment, ethnicity, culture and lifestyle.

(Variations Sub-Group of the Chief Medical Officers Health
of the Nation Working Group 1996: 5)

In the United Kingdom in particular, the report noted evidence of marked
differences by occupational group, region, ethnicity and sex.[8] Elsewhere, in
the Netherlands for example, the greatest contributions to health inequalities are age, education, income and occupation (Ruwaard and Kramers
1998: 63).

In the United States, Verbrugge (1989, 1985) has examined a range of epidemiological evidence to highlight male disadvantage with regard to mortality data and possibly morbidity. Her central theoretical perspective is that sex differences in health derive from differential risks acquired from sex roles, stress, lifestyles and preventive health practices. Less important are psychosocial factors, for example how men and women evaluate symptoms and the concomitant readiness to take therapeutic action. But both sets of risks are perceived to be grounded in a 'biological substrate' (Verbrugge 1989: 296). In the broader context of investigation of men's beliefs and behaviour, social scientists have suggested that men encounter an array of prescriptions and proscriptions through the impact of sex role norms (Kimmel 1987) and gender socialization (Pleck 1981). Congruent with the resultant 'masculinity agenda' are tensions derived from age (Riley 1988) and status (Mortimer 1988), elements identified as being strong social determinants of unhealthy lifestyles (Abel 1991).

There is a further problem in interpreting mortality and morbidity data that derives from a gender bias in the reporting of certain diseases. To take the example of CHD, a health series for women, on Channel 4 television in the United Kingdom, called *Gimme Health*, made the point that men are twice as likely as women to be referred to hospital for treatment for CHD. One reason for this is that, until recently, it was understood to be about 20 times more common in younger men than women (Kannel and Gordon, 1974). This view of CHD as a male disease has informed and been reinforced by major studies of CHD risk factors (Balarajan and McDowell 1988; Lichtenstein *et al.* 1985; Shaper *et al.* 1981) and CHD interventions (WHO European Collaborative Group 1986; Puska *et al.* 1983), which have taken men to be the primary study population. That is, men's experience of CHD, captured through surveys, psychometric testing and other tools of clinical surveillance, has been taken as the norm.

The general point about the normative role that the male plays in the medical and social spheres has also been noted – in the context of a feminist critique of health promotion – by Naidoo and Daykin (1995): 'sexism in medical research and epidemiology has led to the setting of public health priorities, and the development of services, based on the experiences of men' (1995: 65). The use of white middle-class heterosexual men as the reference group against which the health experiences of other population groups can be compared and thus made explicit makes it difficult to separate out men's health as a field of concern. Ekenstam (1998), commenting in a Swedish context, notes that 'masculinity is not only a risk factor in disease aetiology but it's also among the most significant barriers to men developing [self-awareness] about health and illness. Similarly, Lloyd (1996: 9) argues that the literature on gender differences largely fails to investigate why men behave as they do, presenting men as the 'control group' against which to contrast women's attitudes, behaviours and beliefs.

Masculinity, masculinities

In 1988, at Bradford in the UK, a conference called 'Men, masculinity and social theory' was organized by the British Sociological Association. In a subsequent publication of the same title, Hearn and Morgan noted that a common theme among all the papers presented was the relative invisibility of men, as an explicit focus in mainstream research and theory. Kimmel has argued that this may not be entirely accidental in that it keeps men's activities free of critical scrutiny. Nevertheless, feminist research and theory have put men under the spotlight as far as pornography, sexual harassment, violence against women and children, health care and reproduction (to name but a few areas of study) are concerned.

According to Hearn and Morgan (1990), the links between gender and theory may be understood in two ways. First, we can focus on theorizing gender and on the ways in which existing theoretical approaches contribute to or obscure understanding of subjective gender issues. Second, we can see the relationship turned on its head so as to focus on the extent to which gender issues might contribute to a critique of the process of constructing theory itself (Hearn and Morgan 1990: 8). This is taken forward in Chapter 2, in the context of the feminist critique of the construction of scientific knowledge. There is a third way of understanding, however, and that is deriving theory from the bottom up, from the personal everyday experiences and practices of men and women (Frank 1991; Connell 1995; Gottfried 1998). This is a legitimate perspective to adopt if one subscribes to the view that, despite a wealth of clinical, epidemiological and psychological research, health and social care professionals, researchers and policymakers still know very little about how the human male will personally experience health over his lifetime. In particular, how learning to be a man and changing experience of health interact.

Connell has identified four main strategies used to define masculinity: essentialist, positivist, normative and semiotic (see Table 1.4). Exposing the weaknesses in each, he argues that it is from the semiotic opposition of masculinity and femininity – the idea that 'one symbol can only be understood within a connected system of symbols – that the principle of connection has significance i.e. masculinity arises from within a system of gender relations (Connell 1995: 71). This leads him on to the observation that, rather than treating masculinity as an object, we need to look at 'the processes and relationships through which men and women conduct gendered lives' (Connell 1995: 71). In turn, this leads Connell (1995: 71) to formulate a contingent definition of masculinity as 'simultaneously a place in gender relations, the practices through which men and women engage that place in gender, and the effects of these practices in bodily experience, personality and culture'. Masculinity and femininity are 'inherently relational concepts' (Connell 1995: 44), and knowledge of masculinity cannot be acquired

Table 1.4 Connell's typology of strategies used to define masculinity

Strategy	Focus	Example	Weakness
Essentialist	Picking out a defining feature of the masculine	Risk-taker, aggressive, responsible, 'zeus energy'	Choice of essence is arbitrary
Positivist	'What men actually are'	Masculinity/ femininity scales in psychology	• 'No description without a standpoint' • Sex differences in behaviour systematically exaggerated • Does not allow for contradictions within personality
Normative	Social norms	Sex roles e.g. 'the sturdy oak', 'the breadwinner'	• Few men meet these norms • 'What is normative about a norm hardly anyone meets?' • Provides no grip on personality
Semiotic	Gender as a system of symbolic relationships	Psychoanalytic thinking e.g. the phallus as master-signifier	• Social analysis is not just about discourse • Need to look at other kinds of relationships, e.g. gendered places in production and consumption

Source: adapted from Connell (1995: 68–71)

outwith the study of gender relations. But, as several authors (Brod 1987; Segal 1990; Wight 1993; Connell 1995; Seidler 1997)[9] have demonstrated, we need to address the relationships between dominant and subordinate or marginal masculinities (including those outwith the hetero-homosexual axis) as much as the impact of the predominant gender order on women. Arguably, the former is as much a feature of gender relations and thus a requirement of analysis as is the latter.

Consideration of the heterogeneous and dynamic nature of gender relations in general and masculinity in particular is a recent development in the literature on gender theory. Rather, the early focus of work in psychology was around the nature–nurture debate – whether biology determines destiny – and its empirical studies were framed accordingly (Segal 1990: 60). In the 1950s, interest in the sociological category of sex roles developed, underpinned by an assumption that 'the social expectations, rules or norms attached to a person's position in society will usually force individuals to conform to them through processes of positive and negative reinforcement'

(Segal 1990: 65). The impact of feminist thinkers in the 1960s was to shift the focus of study to the social context and conditioning of sex role behaviour (Segal 1990: 62). Connell (1995: 70) exposes the problem with the normative orientation of sex role theory when he asks: 'What is "normative" about a norm hardly anyone meets?' Even so, as Sayers (1986) notes, 'the psychological search for innate *difference* between the sexes continues unabated, even though the main finding of some 80 years research has been the massive psychological *similarity* between the sexes in terms of individual attributes'.

In effect, this research has left us little wiser about the actual demands made on men, or of the political and emotional dynamics of masculinity and, especially, why men are resistant to change (Segal 1990: 69), or subordinate masculinities resist dominant cultural codes (de Certeau 1994). A good example of this can be seen in research on Victorian notions of manliness. The Victorian ideal of manliness took various forms. Earnestness, selflessness and integrity were central to the early Victorian ideal, whilst stoicism, hardiness and endurance denoted late Victorian ideals. But both encompassed the qualities of physical courage, chivalric ideals, virtuous fortitude and, in the context of evolving Victorian imperialism, military and patriotic virtue (Mangan and Walvin 1987) which by the end of the nineteenth century had come together in the cult of muscular Christianity (Mangan and Walvin 1987: 3). Though this was a hegemonic phenomenon and had its mirror image in the Victorian concept of femininity, it has been suggested that both ideals were constrained by the overriding effects of social class and economic reality. For example, attempts to extend the notion of Christian manliness to working-class teenagers through agencies such as the Boys' Brigade (Springhall 1987) and the Boy Scouts (MacKenzie 1987) were only partially successful (mainly with upwardly aspiring upper working-class or lower middle-class parents). The goal of the Boys' Brigade was 'the advancement of Christ's Kingdom among boys and the promotion of habits of Obediance, Reverence, Discipline, Self-respect *and all that tends towards a true Christian Manliness*' (Springhall 1987: 53). However, Springhall argues that such ideals failed to take root in the mass of working-class families because most young working-class men shared a different concept of masculinity. Segal (1990: 110) comes to a similar conclusion when she writes that 'for the majority of young working class men manliness remained synonymous with what their would-be educators described as "hooliganism": the manly was to be reached through swaggering, brawling and the oblivion produced through alcohol or violence'. What such research illustrates is that the concept of manliness, of what it meant to be a man, has never had a simple, coherent meaning. Rather, it is an umbrella term encompassing a variety of overlapping perspectives, in which there may be dominant and dominated, mainstream and marginalized masculinities which emerge and evolve or disappear over time (Mangan and Walvin

1987; Connell 1995). In turn, it is possible to see their impact in the range of cultural messages that, according to Harris (1995), are available to men in constructing gendered identities in the late twentieth century.

The salience of practice

No one would deny that men's health has biological and behavioural aspects. Similarly, masculinity and health have been linked at the level of explanation. The problem is that these are 'part-definitions' (Lloyd 1996: 6). Moreover, in the United Kingdom at least, they have been operationalized around an essentialist view of what it means to be a man (for example: taking risks, being aggressive). This does not facilitate access to an understanding of the personal configuration of health in men's lives. Similarly, whilst gender and risk may be salient as research and policy issues, their relevance in the more immediate context of daily life is questionable (this is an issue that is picked up in Chapter 3). Yet, neither is insight acquired simply from adding in a dose of lay health beliefs, as is advocated as part of the new public health (Long 1993). There is a need to move beyond the fragmented definitions of men's health, and especially the role of masculinity, that currently dominate the admittedly sporadic and tetchy debate around the subject. This requires both a more assured engagement with relevant theory and substantial empirical investigation. The challenge is to discern whether and how masculinity and health operate within daily lives.

In his earlier book on *Gender and Power*, Connell (1987) proposed that existing analyses of gender failed to deal with the element of practical problems – in this instance, with how masculinity(ies) is put together and endures in everyday contexts. This moved Connell (1987: 63) to advocate a focus on practice. Connell is himself drawing on a rich seam of work that began to appear in anthropology in the 1980s – following the publication of Bourdieu's *Outline of a Theory of Practice* (1977) in English – around understanding how society and culture produced and reproduced themselves through human action and interaction. The key symbol of this enterprise, which encompassed a number of theories and methods, was called 'practice', 'praxis' or 'action' by its various exponents (Ortner 1984: 127; see also Giddens 1991).

As early as the 1960s it was being suggested that theory was not irrelevant to the hard practical realities of everyday life, because what is hard or practical is determined by the concepts used and assumptions made (Scott 1969). In his work on social change Mayer (1972) provides another example of the application of a practice-oriented approach to an examination of social problems. He identified two prerequisites: first, a social problem must be identified; then one identifies a system of social relations in which the problem occurs.

Practice theory is about explaining the relationships that obtain between human action and the system and vice versa; the most important forms of which are realized in the context of asymmetrical or dominated relationships (Ortner 1984: 149). Ortner (1984: 157) goes on to suggest that 'to penetrate into the workings of asymetrical social relations is to penetrate to the heart of much of what is going on in any given system'. But this, too, is partial: 'Patterns of cooperation, reciprocity and solidarity constitute the other side of the coin of social being' (Ortner 1984: 157). Put another way, it is about theorizing 'big structures from small acts' (Gottfried 1998: 455).

Connell (1995: 65) says of practice that it never takes place in a vacuum:

> It always responds to a situation and situations are structured in ways that admit certain possibilities and not others. Practice does not proceed into a vacuum either. Practice makes a world. In acting, we convert initial situations into new situations. Practice constitutes and reconstitutes structures . . . It makes the reality we live in.

In different ways this position is reflected in the work of Bourdieu (1977; 1990), Gramsci (1978), Giddens (1991) and de Certeau (1994), the influences of which are acknowledged in the later work of Gottfried (1998) and Connell (1995). The focus on the body and embodiment in this volume is influenced most directly, however, by the work of Merleau-Ponty (1962) and others working in the phenomenological or interpretative tradition (Young 1989; Leder 1992; Csordas 1994; Bendelow and Williams 1995; Connell 1995; Crossley 1995). This literature has served to open up our appreciation of embodiment (to get at practical experience).

Locating masculinity in social practice

In talking about the social organization of masculinity, Connell clearly sets out the analysis of gender that underpins his work. He starts by stating that '[g]ender is a way in which social practice is ordered' (Connell 1995: 71). He goes on to claim that gender is social practice that constantly refers to bodies and what bodies do, but that it is not social practice reduced to bodies (Connell 1995: 71). Gender is said to exist precisely to the extent that biology does not determine the social (a point made in anthropology by Mary Douglas). Social practice is creative and inventive but not without limits. 'It responds to particular situations and is generated within definite structures of social relations' (Connell 1995: 72). Masculinity (or femininity) as a static configuration is not important; rather, Connell asserts that the construction of gendered identity is a project. A project can be defined as a process of configuring practice through time – the process is unfolding or, if you like, unfinished (see also Giddens 1991; Shilling 1993). Relatedly, Rossi (1985), Connell (1995) and Gatens (1996) assert the agency of bodies in social processes. Connell and Gatens argue for a theoretical position in which bodies are seen as sharing in social agency, in generating and shaping courses of conduct. The body is not a finished product, mechanical and unreasoning; rather, *pace* Descartes, it is a process and its meanings and capacities will varying according to its context (Gatens 1996: 57). Connell (1995) mirrors this position when he notes, quite vividly, that in 1994 there were around 5.4 thousand million bodies, each with its own trajectory through time, each one changing as it grows and ages, engulfed in and sustained by social processes that are also certain to change.

In a sense, and reflecting this point, any one masculinity, as a configuration of practice, is simultaneously positioned in a number of structures of relationships, which may be following different historical and cultural trajectories. So Connell proposes a threefold model of the structure of gender. This model focuses on the dynamic interaction of relations of power (the overall subordination of women and dominance of men – patriarchy), production (gender divisions of labour are familiar in the form of allocation of tasks, but this also brings with it economic consequences, hence the existence in many businesses of a glass ceiling and the uncosted nature of domestic (family) work) and cathexis (or emotional attachment) (Connell 1995: 74). Connell is less clear when talking of this last dimension. Essentially, he is saying that the practices that shape and realize desire (whether heterosexual or homosexual) are an aspect of the gender order, and that this leads to questions about the consensual or coercive nature of a given relationship.

In sum, Connell argues that we can find the gender configuring of practice however we slice the social world and whatever unit of analysis we choose – for example, the lifecourse (the focus of most psychoanalytic work), discourse (the Foucauldian concern with discourses of knowledge/power and the social ordering of populations; see especially the collection of essays in Petersen and Bunton 1997) and embodiment (Watson *et al.* 1996; Nettleton and Watson 1998b).

A crucial point about this model is that gender is positioned as a general means of structuring social practice and not as a specific form of practice. Gender interacts with other social structures such as race and class (Connell 1995; Gottfried 1998). For example, white men's masculinities are constructed not only in relation to white women but also in relation to black men. Similarly, an ideal of working-class manliness and self-respect was constructed in response to class deprivation and paternalistic strategies of management. Connell's point is that to understand gender we must constantly go beyond gender.

A good example of the kind of research required can be found in Mullen (1993). It is an insightful contribution to the literature on lay health knowledge, though Mullen uses the term 'beliefs'. In this book Mullen considers the role of social class and religion in the lives of Glaswegian men, paying particular attention to the occupational and lifestyle elements of social class, and to the relationship between control and responsibility for health drawn from the religious and moral elements of respondent accounts. For example, the relationship between activity and health is tied to respondents' conceptualizations of work and occupation. In particular, Mullen argues in a work context, that even if smoking and drinking alcohol are bad for physical health, they may still serve a purpose when employed to help manage the pressures of work. The coping strategies employed by his respondents range from reactive and self-contradictory compensation strategies to proactive attempts to control the work environment.

As Mullen's analysis develops, the centrality of the dichotomy of control and release, the latter circumscribed to a limited range of options around tobacco and alcohol use, emerges. These twin concepts were first presented by Crawford (1984). Mullen shows the difficulties that participants had in 'balancing both sides of the dichotomy' and thereby maximizing their chances of good health. He demonstrates that for his participants the 'balancing' of contrasting positions between moderation and excess is achievable through marriage, fatherhood and religion, which provide alternatives to smoking and drinking 'and draw people towards responsible conviviality' (Mullen 1993: 177).

As a sociological account of health and illness, Mullen's preoccupation was with the cognitive and structural dimensions of experience. As such, it delved into the practical everyday choices and constraints that men have to grapple with. However, it also illustrates another element of Connell's analysis, that is, that we also need to focus on the gender relations among men, relations often founded upon the realities of asymmetrical power relations – specifically, how his informants dealt with institutionalized forms of hegemony and complicity with the hegemonic project. Marriage, fatherhood and work often involve extensive compromises with women and between different constellations of masculinities rather than outright domination, marginalization of subordinated classes or ethnic groups.

More recently, research with a group of working-class men experiencing long-term unemployment (Willott and Griffin 1997) used discourse analysis to explore the narrative patterns constructed by these men in their efforts to retain their position within hegemonic discourses of masculinity. They found that masculine identities were constructed with reference to breadwinning and public consumption. The former concept is often cited as a pervasive and powerful element of masculine identity (Harris 1995) and, as noted earlier, may be reflected in masculine conceptions of health (Kristiansen 1989). Relatedly, Wight (1993: 139) comments that '[g]ender categories were probably those most clearly expressed and reproduced by means of consumption; whether the commodities used . . . who used them . . . or the division of consumer tasks'. But, as he goes on to say, the main role of the man in his family was to provide them with the means to consume 'and their standard of living was the principal way in which his responsibility to them was judged' (Wight 1993: 141). In this context, unemployed men might talk of 'fiddling' as a form of work/survival, not only reasonable given their circumstances but the only assertive form of action available (Wilott and Griffin 1997: 122).

The critical step that Connell urges us to take, and which some of the literature referred to above illustrates, is that understanding 'a historical process of this depth and complexity [i.e. changes in gender relations] is not a task for *a priori* theorising. It requires concrete study(ies) to illuminate the larger dynamic' (Connell 1995: 86). Relatedly, Gottfried (1998: 465) argues that 'an excavation of lived practices can make visible the gendering process and ground analysis of specific forms of male power in relationship to class and other heirarchies'.

Arguably, the social location *par excellence* for this excavation is the body. Many of the concerns of men and masculinities are directly to do with bodies – sport (think of football and boxing) and war (the opening scenes of Spielberg's film, *Saving Private Ryan*) are obvious examples. By contrast, Gagnon (1974) argues that in the late twentieth century '[m]an's body as the primary tool in shaping the world is nearly obsolete and the distinctions between men that were created on the base of it have lost their validity'. Gagnon's stance, though, is somewhat undermined by the persistence of powerful 'representations' of the desirable male body. For example, a strand of psychological research over the past four decades has used mainly male college students to explore the desirability and role of body form – mesomorph, ectomorph and endomorph. In particular, such research has investigated relationships between: body form and behaviour (Brodsky 1954; Montemayor 1978); body image stereotypes and body-type preferences (Dibiase and Hjelle 1968); body cathexis and self-esteem (Mahoney 1974); satisfaction with physical appearance (Mishkind *et al.* 1987); and body type and sophistication of body concept (Sugerman and Haronian 1964). This research has demonstrated, at least with its limited representational sampling, that the mesomorphic ideal still has a powerful exemplar role for the American collegiate male.

Easthope (1986) has also demonstrated the continuing role of the mesomorphic male body shape as being a repository of valued masculine characteristics such as courage, tenacity, honesty and even (same/opposite) sex appeal in popular media culture. Elsewhere, in his review of empirical mass media communication research on masculinity, Fejes (1992) has argued that 'men, as portrayed on adult television, do not deviate much from the traditional patriarchal notion of men and masculinity'. Whilst Saco (1992) has argued that '[t]he symbolic sign system within which masculinity and femininity are coded oppositions . . . is what makes the constitution of masculine and feminine subjects possible'. The key point made by such research is that it is the body (and particular body 'representations') that acts as the common ground for the mediation of such meanings. Nevertheless, one should not take such representations or images – even if so powerful – for granted. In particular, it would be a mistake to suggest that the mesomorphic ideal is the only thing that concerns men or to equate such images with practical everyday experience.

For example, Higate's (1998) autobiographical account of life as a clerk in the Royal Air Force demonstrates how bodily control was used, consciously and unconsciously, to undermine the regulated bodily movements required within a military context. Most vividly, though, it captures the tensions and paradoxes contained within the hierarchy of masculinities in which 'clerks' bodies' inhabit a feminine domain in a hypermasculine world. What Higate (1988: 193) says is that 'the body was utilised as a resource [providing] loosely and spontaneously organised pathways to relative autonomy and control'. For example, through intentional acts of bodily betrayal such as suddenly collapsing to the floor, the clerks, although a disempowered and subordinated group, both challenge the social order and foster identity (*esprit de corps*!). This illustrates what Connell (1995: 242) terms 'the differences and tensions between hegemonic and complicit masculinities; oppositions between hegemonic and subordinated and marginalised masculinities'.

Summary

The gender analysis adopted by the Women's Health and Development Programme (WHO 1998b) has gender equity as its goal. However, the analysis is partial since: masculinity is treated as an undifferentiated construct; it is presumed that all men benefit equally from being male in a patriarchal system; and it assumes a deficits rather than an assets perspective of masculinity.

A challenge is to elaborate the theoretical links between constructions of the body and bodily processes in society and constructions of gender and gender identities that may be embedded within everyday accounts. Rossi (1985), Hearn and Morgan (1990), Segal (1990) and Connell (1995) all argue in their various ways that we need to direct the study of gender and masculinities away from the ideological and the cultural towards the bodily without falling into the trap of biological reductionism. This theme of the body is taken up in the following chapter, which explores how the body has been treated by social theorists and critically assesses the contribution of social theorizing to understanding the body in everyday life.

Notes

1 Preliminary investigation of population health data in Sweden (Danielsson *et al.* 1996) suggests that excess male mortality across the life-span existed as far back as the late eighteenth century.

2 At the time the main qualitative study took place, the life expectancy of a Scots-man at birth in 1992 was 71.4 years, lower than that in any other industrialized country except Portugal. What is striking is the existence of a significant male/female difference in life expectancy at birth in all of these countries.

3 The data presented in this chapter are necessarily limited and it is important to acknowledge that a preoccupation with men and health intersects with other factors that affect health outcomes across the population (DoH 1995: 5).

4 At younger ages, it is more difficult to interpret the differences. At ages 20–24, two-thirds of deaths were allocated to a social class, rising to over four-fifths by ages 30–44 and nine-tenths at ages 35–39 (Drever and Bunting 1997: 99).

5 By 1997, it was reported that accidents and suicides were accounting for 47% of deaths in young men aged 15–34 (SODoH 1998a: 37) while mortality from suicide and undetermined injury had increased since the 1970s in all social classes except social class I, where it fell (Drever and Bunting 1997: 106).

6 It should be noted that there were no changes in reporting practices for suicide in Scotland in the period from 1971–73 to 1991–93.

7 At the time of writing this book the new Labour government had commissioned an independent inquiry on inequalities in health from Sir Donald Acheson, a former chief medical officer for the United Kingdom.

8 It is important to be clear about the use of the terms sex and gender in the remainder of this book. Sex is used to refer to the genetically determined and biologically maintained physical differences between the sexes (male and female). By contrast, gender refers to 'women's and men's roles and responsibilities that are socially determined. Gender is related to how we are perceived and expected to act as women and men because of the way society is organized, not because of . . . biological differences' (WHO 1998b: 10).

9 Although space precludes a detailed review, Segal (1990) and Connell (1995) provide a good overall discussion of the construction of masculinity. The former is good on motifs of masculinity, and the latter is strong on the embodiment of masculinity. A more interdisciplinary perspective can be found in Brod (1987), while Seidler (1997) develops his earlier work on the embodiment of reason. Wight (1993) provides an anthropological account of the construction of working-class masculinity.

CHAPTER 2

SOCIAL THEORY, THE BODY AND HEALTH

As the previous chapter highlights, current debate around men's health, and perhaps men's place in society, is crippled by the lack of attention paid to personal accounts and perceptions of maleness. The irony is that whilst we have moved towards a richer and subtler appreciation of women's health over the lifecourse – a reassessment founded partly in the context of lay experience – one might argue men have come to be defined, even constrained, both by their physiology and related behavioural characteristics. In this respect, Connell (1995: 45) notes that 'true masculinity' is almost always thought to proceed from men's bodies: 'the body drives and directs action' (aggression and sex feed off testosterone) or 'sets limits to action' (men do not naturally take care of young children).

Treated thus, the male body has a narrow and partial presence. The knowledge and understanding that flow from this arguably contribute to normative constructions of the male body and behaviour which 'are disempowering at the level of individual experience of the body' (Watson *et al.* 1996: 170). Working against this there has been a growing interest in the embodied nature of the individual (Scott and Morgan 1993; Nettleton and Watson 1998b). It is an epistemological conviction regarding the centrality of the embodied basis of being – historicized, problematic and pragmatic – to our understanding of lay experiences, as described in the Introduction (and in more detail in Chapter 5), that provides a critical location for men's health practices. In order to establish this space, however, it is first necessary to address critically how the body has previously occupied this location.

What this does not amount to is a comprehensive review. Such a task is beyond the scope of this book and has been accomplished far better by others (notably by Featherstone *et al.* 1991; Shilling 1993; Falk 1994 and Williams and Bendelow 1998). Rather, the review focuses initially on the role of metaphor in sacred and scientific discourse in establishing the body as the primary site of a broader social order. This is followed by a critique of that social theorizing about 'the body' which *a priori* assumed the primacy of structure over agency and the social over the biological.

The body as metaphor

The organic machine

In order to identify the body it is necessary to clarify what we mean when we talk of the 'body'. In the English language, as Turner (1992) observes, there is no special term or phrase for the lived body, apart from the notion of embodiment which is largely confined to academic debate and which will be explored later. Rather, the *Oxford English Dictionary* describes the body as

> *n.* **1.** the structure of bones, flesh, etc., of a human being or animal, living or dead. **2.** a corpse, a carcass. **3.** the trunk, the main part of a body apart from the head and limbs . . . **5.** a person . . . **7.** a distinct piece of matter; an object in space . . .

In English, then, to talk of the body is to refer to parts of a whole, or to an abstract whole. In part, this reflects the divided nature of the body in Western culture. This has persisted from the Orphic myth of creation, through Descartes' notion of the human organism as consisting of the palpable body and the intangible mind. It has been a significant feature of scientific discourse, whether empirically or theoretically based, since the Renaissance.

In Western science the status and nature of the body have been most influentially defined by Descartes. In essence, Descartes posed the existence of two types of substance that together comprised the human organism. These were the palpable body and the intangible mind. Writing in the late 1930s, Elias (1978) described this as the individual ' "ego" in a closed case'. Descartes was drawing, perhaps unconsciously, on one of the foundation myths of Western culture, the Orphic myth of creation. It is the Orphic myth, rather than the Adamic myth of 'the fall from grace', which more clearly reflected the metaphorical relation of the soul, and – one might argue – the body, to the cosmos as it was perceived in pre-Renaissance Europe.

Ricoeur (1969) describes the Orphic myth in his study of the symbolism of evil. Essentially, the Orphic myth is a narrative about how the body and the soul, which had separate existences, were united by an event (the Creation) which, Ricoeur (1969: 280) says, inaugurated 'the humanity of man and makes man a place of forgetting'. The soul embodies the remaining essence of a divine being, whilst the body represents the punishment of the divine being's murderers. The divine being, his totality destroyed, survives in essence through existence in the body. The soul is exiled from its rightful place in the cosmos and cannot regain unity with the divine except through temporary earthly existence, which itself is the vehicle for reincorporating into the divine.

This myth is one of several that describe the separation of man from God. Human existence is founded on its dualistic nature: body and soul. From this man perceives himself as the same as his soul and other than his body. The punishment of the body is temporal corruption and hence, given its short-term existence, the body becomes a factor affecting the nature of the individual who is thus predisposed to immediate gratification of bodily desires. Ignorant of his spiritual antecedents, man employs his rationality to achieve such gratification (for an excellent scholarly account of the struggle between body and soul, see Sawday 1995, especially Chapter 2).

When seen in the context of this account of the impact of the Orphic myth, the separation of mind and body by Descartes gave ethical legitimacy to subsequent developments in the natural and clinical sciences. The principal legacy was of a deterministic and mechanistic conception of the body and its functions (Scheper-Hughes and Lock 1987). Indeed, the opening words of Descartes' *Treatise of Man* are: 'I assume their body to be but a statue, an earthen machine . . .' (Beaune 1989). It is from the time of the Renaissance that Beaune (1989: 433) identifies the appearance of the mechanistic automaton which itself is an attempt to dissect and copy the human body.

If the body had its place in a cosmological hierarchy it also served as the site for a number of critical secular relationships. Historically, there have been two major approaches to the body in Western culture. From the time of the classical Greeks to the late seventeenth century, men and women were thought to share the same basic anatomical structure and physiological processes. This one-sex body was, however, the site of a number of critical cultural, social and political oppositions: fatherhood/motherhood, male/female, man/woman, culture/nature, masculine/feminine, honourable/dishonourable, and hot/cold (Laqueur 1990). Women were simply imperfect men, in whom the anatomical structures and physiological balances are lacking due to too much heat being generated at the moment of conception. 'To be a man or a woman was to hold a social rank, a place in society, to assume a cultural role, not to be organically one or the other of two incommensurable sexes' (Laqueur 1990: 8).

Laqueur cites a number of examples to demonstrate his argument about the one-sex body being the site of a number of important oppositions that were, in themselves, ways of expressing hierarchies in the wider society. The 'one-flesh discourse', as Laqueur describes his argument, was quite flexible and able to incorporate the new anatomical knowledge and naturalistic forms of representation that emerged out of the Renaissance period in Europe. If anything, the proliferation of anatomical illustrations strengthened the notion that the body was a 'male' body.

Jordonova (1989) is more explicitly concerned with the ways in which images of male and female bodies carry assumptions about sex roles. Her central thesis is that during the eighteenth and nineteenth centuries 'realism [in depicting the body] was an important goal towards which writers, artists and medical practitioners worked' (Jordonova 1989: 46). For her, this realism is realized in the form and function of wax anatomical models of the nineteenth century. These, she argues, had their basis in an 'anti-mechanistic organic physiology' which itself developed due to a number of interrelated factors clustered around the impact of layering as a concept in the physical (geology) and organic (anatomy) sciences (Jordonova 1989: 56–7). The purpose of the wax model was to convey 'depth' through the study of organ systems and the interior of organisms.

Jordonova, like Illich, acknowledges that bodies and their images are epoch-specific. According to Illich (1986): 'As the body takes shape, we are able to understand how each historical movement is incarnated in an epoch-specific body. We now begin to decipher the body of subjective experience as a unique enfleshment of an age's ethos.'

As alluded to previously, in the nineteenth century middle-class notions of manliness and morality were embodied in a concern with form, function, and development of the body through physical education and athletic sport (Park 1987). This attention to action through the medium of the male body was accompanied by a shift in social and moral values ascribed to various body forms. The lean and lithe ectomorph shape of the eighteenth century gave way to the current cultural ideal of the 'more balanced' and desirable mesomorphic ideal (Park 1987: 10). In this the role of the public school became to instil a new idea of manhood and masculine values based on 'physical fitness, courage and audacity' (Segal 1990). This was a basis on which men went out into the social world. Participation in sport and physical activity was a rite of passage for some young men.

The medicalized body

What appears to have caused the classical approach to the body to break down was that from the late seventeenth century anatomists began to see, and present, a distinct female anatomy (Lawrence and Bendixen 1992). However, Laqueur argues that this change was not led by the anatomists, but rather emerged from two broader historical conjunctions. The first of these was epistemological in that the body was no longer universally viewed as 'a microcosm of some larger social order'; the new biology was concerned with a search for fundamental differences between the sexes (Laqueur 1990). This epistemological development coincided with the major revolutionary upheavals at the end of the seventeenth century and the start of the eighteenth century. This 'modern' approach to the body was not a radical departure from the classical approach, in that its foundations were still predicated upon the male body as the standard anatomical form. Rather, the female anatomy was compared with the male norm in order to establish the biological difference of women. Thus the one-sex model was replaced by a two-sex model: 'A biology of cosmic hierarchy gave way to a biology of incommensurability, anchored in the body, in which the relationship of men to women was not given as one of equality or inequality but rather of difference' (Laqueur 1990: 207).

The body in the eighteenth and nineteenth centuries was inscribed by gendered polarities in anatomy and pathology, for example the feminization of the nervous system and the masculinization of the musculature. Jordonova (1989: 59) states that '[d]isequilibrated social relations have frequently been signalled by a language of gendered anatomy and pathology'. She goes on to argue (Jordonova 1989: 138) that medical and scientific images of the body were gendered in order to impose order and differentiation between the sexes at a time of political and social upheaval. More importantly, such gendered representations of the human body were used as 'natural' bases from which other attributes of masculinity and femininity could be added. Gender, read into individual bodies, becomes a central medical metaphor and from this basis of difference society is structured, being implicated in the distinctions and boundaries between healthy and unhealthy, clean and dirty, pure and defiled, man and woman. Jordonova (1989: 139), quoting Mary Douglas, opines that these boundaries 'express the very heart of a society . . . its cosmology and its social structure'.

In a recent review of anatomy texts used by US medical students between 1890 and 1989, Lawrence and Bendixen (1992) found that the texts they examined had generally remained consistent in how the human body has been depicted. In both illustrations and text, the male anatomy was usually depicted as the standard against which female structures are compared. Clearly, then, the modern anatomical texts they examined have continued the historical conventions of the classical and modern periods in which the male anatomy is the basic model for the human body.

The essence of the modern gendered body was its seeming essentialism, the naturalization of sexual and social status that it facilitated. Herzlich and Pierret (1987: 69) describe this process thus: 'Historically . . . the reading of the body has become more circumscribed, because the suffering flesh, the shapeless body of the sick person, has now become the object of knowledge and the space of disease'. More importantly for a study around masculinity and health, 'the body became the locus of norms par excellence' (Herzlich and Pierret 1987: 152), both moral and social.

This exemplification of the body, and particularly female bodies, as the site of medical appropriation and practice is explored by Martin (1989). She explores the different ways by which menstruation, childbirth and menopause are perceived, contrasting medical and lay accounts of these processes. From her examination of medical texts she poses the question of how women respond to scientific metaphors about their bodies within the contexts of their everyday lives (Martin 1989: 67). She demonstrates that the (female) body had become fragmented and objectified through its appropriation by medical science.

Earlier, mention was made of how gender became a central medical metaphor. Martin shows how a (male) Western medical profession has drawn upon metaphors of production and alienation, in turn, to explain key female bodily processes. In effect, she argues for the existence of a dominant male ideology of women's bodies in medical textbooks and practice, an ideology apparent in the representation of human anatomical structures reported by Lawrence and Bendixen. This gendered perspective is most clearly articulated when she considers the lay accounts of the women who took part in her study regarding images of self and body, and compares them with the medical corpus referred to previously.

For example, her analysis of the differences between objectified technical medical descriptions of the process of childbirth and those subjective accounts articulated by women in her study shows a strong tension between the two types of account. This tension originates in the nature and function of those asymmetrical, dominating relationships that characterize attempts by a 'male' medical profession to impose order particularly on female bodies, and contemporary resistance to this process among women. Martin is not, however, adopting a pure social constructionist perspective on the validity or otherwise of the medical knowledge of childbirth; rather, participant accounts are sometimes contextualized in the physiological reality of bodily change but in forms that describe very different ways of interpreting this reality. Physiological reality is not dismissed, it is reworked. In this respect, the interesting anthropological question for Martin (1989: 195) is 'how we draw the line between aspects of science that are part of the taken-for-granted nature of reality – the earth exists – and aspects that assume a view of the world that might well be different'.

More recently, Alexanderson et al. (1998) examined the issue of gender bias in a range of medical textbooks currently used in Sweden in the fields of dermatology, epidemiology, occupational medicine and public health. Their study confirmed the gender bias found by other researchers (Martin 1989; Lawrence and Bendixen 1992; Mendelsohn et al. 1994) in which the male is usually the norm, or reference point, to which the female body is compared. Ironically, they suggest that the mainly male authors of the textbooks reviewed had 'striven to describe a gender neutrality that is not real' rather than acknowledging the differences that affect the health of men and women (Alexanderson *et al.* 1998: 159).

Feminist criticism of scientific discourse

At this point it is worth setting Martin's critique within the broader thrust of a feminist critique of the ways in which knowledge of the (female) body has been constructed. Contemporary feminist thought, particularly among those who have developed critiques of biological determinist theories of human behaviour and their modern equivalent – sociobiological theory – start from the assumption that Western science is genderized. Keller (1985) has argued that Western science is underpinned by a basic congruence between maleness, as culturally defined, and the prevailing scientific worldview. That is:

> The relationship between knower and known is one of distance and separation . . . between a subject and object radically divided . . . nature objectified. The characterisation of both the scientific mind and its modes of access to knowledge as masculine is . . . significant. Masculine here connotes . . . autonomy, separation, and distance.
>
> (Keller 1985: 414–15)

Bleir (1984), arguing that scientific discourse on the nature of men and women is socially constructed and genderized, comments that dualisms such as subject/object, knower/known, male/female and nature/culture have also structured investigation into and the perceptions of 'the way human beings think, behave, and organise themselves'. A particular feature of this process has, for Bleir (1984: 76), been the way in which women have come to be defined, even constrained by their biology. According to Nead (1992), this notion of containment is reflected in the Western high art tradition in which

> [w]oman is both 'mater' (mother) and 'materia' (matter), biologically determined and potentially wayward . . . The question of containment and boundaries is thus a critical one in representations of the female body. The integrity of the female figure is guaranteed by the impenetrability of its framing contours.

Perhaps Martin's (1989) most provocative comment sums up the consequences of this treatment of the female body: 'women are not only fragmented into body parts by the practices of scientific medicine, as men are; they are also profoundly alienated from science itself'.

She then goes on to cite Keller (1985) by saying that women are less involved in the production of science as a form of cultural activity because of 'a network of interactions between gender development, a belief system that equates objectivity with masculinity, and a set of cultural values that . . . elevates what is defined as scientific and what is defined as masculine'. In addition, the content of science presents 'a male-biased model of human nature and social reality' (Jagger 1983). Martin's presentation of the argument at this point is flawed. A few lines later she claims that her central task is to confront 'the claims about our cultural representations' with the empirical data that she had gathered (Martin 1989). Yet that task is itself informed by assumptions that men are not as profoundly alienated from science as women are.

By contrast, Dinnerstein (1976) and Chodorow (1978) have argued that the containment of women is a consequence of the development of flexible ego boundaries which leave the self 'open' and as one with the world. By contrast, men have more rigid ego boundaries which enable the self to be separate from others. The process of developing a social persona distinct from one's physical form appears, from analysis of the data, to be a process that is coterminous with the development of gendered roles and obligations. In a sociological and feminist treatment of mothering, Chodorow (1978: 169) identifies a process within the development of male gender of the forming of rigid boundaries between the male self and others:

> From the retention of pre-oedipal attachments to their mother, growing girls come to define and experience themselves as continuous with others; their experience of self contains more flexible or permeable ego boundaries. Boys come to define themselves as more separate and distinct, with a greater sense of rigid ego boundaries and differentiation . . . the basic masculine sense of self is separate.

This view is reflected in the writing of Fasteau (1974) who, echoing Beaune's notion of the automaton, employs the metaphor of 'the male machine' to describe the American male – a 'machine' which, by its own separateness, confronts the world in which it exists. This strand of American sociological thought is profoundly pessimistic in its assessment of the impact of gender categorization on the structural fabric of everyday life. Overall, the main point of the feminist critique of the dichotomization of knowledge is that culture and, within that, gender are ultimately, and inevitably, constraining.

Social theorizing of 'the body'

Until the appearance of Turner's *The Body and Society* (1984), at least in English-speaking countries, sociology, on the whole, denied the importance of physical, physiological and genetic factors in human social life (Scott and Morgan 1993). In part, this may have been driven by a contempt for sociobiology and social Darwinism, but it was also a historical result of the development of sociology. Durkheim claimed the 'social' (or 'cultural') for sociology, and his descendants still seem to be fighting for autonomy from biological imperialism (Hurst and Woolley 1982; Strong 1986). This is fascinating since it ignores the history of the body as a cultural, material and scientifically mediated form.

However, human attributes, instead of being missing entirely from the discipline, have formed the basis of many social theories according to the 'absent presence' ideas of Shilling (1993). This omission of the body has resulted in a social or cultural essentialism that has produced an unsatisfactory conception of social relations. Given the discipline's historical antecedents, then, the recent growth of a sociology of the body seems surprising. Social scientists writing in the mid-1980s could deplore the neglect of the body in social theory. Since then, a stream of books, monographs and articles have reclaimed the body, problematized it and created for it a central place within social theory. The importance of a theoretical understanding of the body in furthering sociological and cultural analysis of issues such as health and illness, sexuality, identity and power in contemporary society should not be underestimated. However, whilst this new-found interest is to be welcomed, there are a number of problems with the current state of sociology of the body, derived primarily from the twin influences of Foucault and feminism. Certainly these twin influences, whilst not mutually exclusive, do go some way towards explaining the wide divergence of work in this area. Both, in their way, have stimulated and framed a generation of research, but as enterprises they can be accused of elevating social determinism to a par with biological determinism. This charge is founded upon three critical points regarding sociology of the body.[1] These are that it has: privileged theorizing of 'the body'; bracketed out the individual; and largely ignored practical experiences of embodiment.

Some problems with social theory

One can start by stating the obvious. Sociology of the body has been theoretically driven, with little empirical research available in the published literature. As Scott and Morgan (1993: 12) have argued: 'Theory may admit the body but the theorist remains disembodied'. In one of the few articles in the journal *Body and Society* that presents findings from a qualitative study, Wacquant (1995: 65) makes the following point:

the newer sociology of the body has paid surprisingly little focused attention to the diverse ways in which specific social worlds invest, shape, and deploy human bodies and to the concrete incorporating practices whereby their social structures are effectively embodied by the agents who partake of them.

Sociology of the body merely appears to be presenting the body as text, in the same way that the body is represented as a line drawing or photograph in anatomy (Armstrong 1983; Lawrence and Bendixen 1992) or depicted in art (Nead 1992; Stafford 1995). Certainly the physical body has been appropriated as a theoretical context for either the explication of its symbolic properties (Douglas 1982, 1988) or the fashioning and inscription of the body through discourse (Foucault 1973, 1979; Arney and Neill 1982; Armstrong 1983; Nettleton 1988).

For example, the notion of the body as a site for the social control of the individual has been most challengingly developed in the work of Michel Foucault, particularly in *The Birth of the Clinic* (Foucault 1973) and *Discipline and Punish* (Foucault 1979). In these, as in his other works, Foucault has investigated the forms of knowledge and the institutions that have controlled and integrated modern societies since the eighteenth century. In *Discipline and Punish*, he analyses the emergence of institutional and cognitive techniques of control – the control of bodies in time and space – through the medium of the disciplining of the body by the social organization of the Panopticon. For example, asylums and prisons began to emerge as a feature of social control in the late eighteenth century, in which 'a body had no existence prior to its crystallisation in the space delineated by a monitoring gaze' (Armstrong 1983: 5). In *The Birth of the Clinic*, it is the display and representation of bodies through the emergence and ascendancy of anatomy, the medical appropriation and control of knowledge – and hence power – in relation to bodies, that is a central focus. As with *Discipline and Punish*, bodies are constituted under the monitoring gaze – of the doctor. Armstrong (1983: 43) extended this analysis to what he describes as the disciplines of the survey – the examination of bodies via the dispensary, the epidemiological survey and general practice, which 'involved the approximation and comparison of each body with the "normal"'.

Armstrong has drawn into focus the implications of Foucault's approach to knowledge with respect to the relationship between biology and sociology. With reference to the biological principles which have provided a fundamental basis – or unchallenged pre-given – for the social theorizing of Parsons and Giddens, he writes that

> [h]uman anatomy has maintained its hegemony over sociology for too long . . . Surely it is now time to challenge the cognitive ordering of a field of knowledge held under the suzerainty of anatomy. It is time to . . . grasp the possibilities for different configurations of knowledge.
> (Armstrong 1987: 65)

Other sociologists have taken up this challenge. For example, Nettleton (1988, 1989) has challenged the nature of dental knowledge derived from empirical and pluralistic accounts of the development of the modern discipline of dentistry. By contrast, she has argued that: (i) 'the mouth and its attendant disease only became part of our reality once it was perceived', that is, knowledge of the mouth became separated from knowledge of the rest of the body, through its perception by dentists (Nettleton 1988: 158); (ii) the need for dental care was created through 'a process of normalisation ... which incorporated a whole series of techniques of knowledge that created a new region of dental disease through the conception of dental health' (Nettleton 1988: 159); (iii) the 'practices of prevention, through its techniques of surveillance [the monitoring gaze] ... produced knowledge of mouths' (Nettleton 1988: 159). It was through these processes that dentistry became established as a medical profession. Elsewhere, Arney and Neill (1982) have proposed a Foucauldian genealogy for the emergence of obstetrics, whilst Arney and Bergen (1983) have proposed a similar genealogy of knowledge for the transformation and treatment of disability.

Similarly, the practice of health education, concerned as it is with promoting a 'regime' of healthy behaviours (healthy eating, exercise, drinking sensibly and managing stress) and seeking to eliminate unhealthy behaviours (excess eating, smoking, and excess drinking), has been likened in recent sociological enquiry to society seeking to impose control over individuals and 'order' populations through the promotion of specific forms of health behaviour aimed at controlling bodies (Beattie 1991; Bunton 1992). On this basis, one might construct a genealogy of knowledge to account for the emergence of health education. However, Foucault might argue that the practice of health education is more concerned with instilling 'technologies of the self' than the overt exercise of power by the state and medical disciplines (Foucault 1988). Certainly, such technologies appear to be elemental in the dietary regimes described by Schwartz (1986) and Hughes (1992).

McNay (1992) has argued that although the treatment of the body as a cultural rather than a natural entity creates an opening for a feminist critique of patriarchy and male power, there are limits to Foucault's idea of the body. For example, she argues that in his earlier works the emphasis placed upon the effects of power on the body reduces social agents to passive bodies. There is no explanation in this for how the individual may act in an autonomous fashion. McNay acknowledges that his development of the concept of techniques of the self is a means through which individuals actively fashion their own identities. However, she argues that this represents not a rejection of Enlightenment values, but an attempt to rework some of its central categories, such as the interrelated concepts of autonomy and emancipation (McNay 1992: 5).

In some respects, Foucauldian discourse mirrors the concerns of Douglas and others in establishing boundaries between regulated and unregulated areas of human activity. Hutton (1988) has argued that this 'creates a mentality that interprets such activity in terms of binary oppositions:

sanity:insanity, health:illness . . .'. In this respect, the techniques of the self are the means by which individuals participate in their own surveillance – monitoring their own behaviour.

The literature that has been reviewed so far in this chapter articulates, or can be viewed from, a social perspective. In this sense, the physical body has, over the past 20-odd years, been appropriated as a theoretical context for either the explication of symbolical representations of the body or the fashioning and inscription of the body through discourse. Such approaches, particularly the latter, are important because they illuminate something of the way in which existing institutions and disciplines fashion their own knowledge/reality and, hence, produce and wield power.

However, a complete reliance on them as a basis on which to approach the body has limitations. The bodies they construct are complaisant – unsubstantiated as having a material existence of their own. This tells the observer little of the way in which individuals experience the world from their perspectives. In a sense, much of this theorizing is two-dimensional, being concerned with the surfaces of bodies. Social theorizing has tended to ignore the interior spaces of the body and the interdependent and contingent nature of relations between exterior and interior spaces – of the lived body. The reading of the body as a social entity is a restricted one that would benefit from being opened up. As Shilling (1993: 10–11) says:

> to achieve an adequate analysis of the body we need to regard it as a material, physical and biological phenomenon which is irreducible to immediate social processes or classifications. Furthermore, our senses, knowledgeability and capability to act are integrally related to the fact that we are embodied beings . . . Human bodies are taken up and transformed as a result of living in society, but they remain material, physical and biological entities.

This brings us to the second element of the argument, that sociology of the body brackets out the individual. The embodied individual is seen primarily as a site for the investment of social order – the Durkheimian project of regulating the social collectivity. In social theory this project has been articulated through the medium of two major and related typologies of the body (Turner 1984; Frank 1991) and in anthropology through the work of Mary Douglas (1982, 1988). A common binding theme that appears to operate, whether at the level of symbolism or discourse, is that of the Durkheimian concern with the regulation of the social collectivity. In social theory this has been articulated in the context of two major and related typologies of the body developed by Turner (1984) and Frank (1991). Each of these typologies is discussed briefly in turn.

The essence of Turner's (1984) typology is that all social systems must resolve the problem of the body. To this end,

[a] sociology of the body is a study of the problem of social order and it can be organised around four issues. These are the reproduction and regulation of populations in time and space, and the restraint and representation of the body as a vehicle for the self.

Turner argues that these four issues, which correspond to an internal/external division, that is, between the body of populations and the body of individuals, are predicated upon the assumption of key dichotomies in Western society. These dichotomies have been discussed above, but for Turner include: private/public and female/male. Consequently, for Turner (1984), a sociology of the body involves an analysis of 'how certain cultural polarities are politically enforced through the institutions of sex, family and patriarchy'.

Frank (1991) has argued that this typology views the body 'from the perspective of the society, society's tasks, its problems of government'. Whilst acknowledging that Turner's categories of reproduction, restraint, regulation and representation enable the ordering of empirical data about the body in society, he suggests that this locates the body as a functional problem for society which limits Turner's approach as a basis for a sociology of the body. Instead, Frank starts from the perspective of the body as a problem for itself. Rather than being a system problem (functional), the body in Frank's typology is viewed as an action problem (phenomenological) (Frank 1991: 47). His rationale for this approach is that '[b]odies alone have "tasks"' (Frank 1991: 48); society provides the context for these tasks. The tasks that Frank (1991: 51–2) identifies for the body are:

- *control* – assessing how predictable its performance will be;
- *desire* – assessing whether the body lacks or is producing desires;
- *relation to others* – whether the body relates to itself (monadic) or to others (dyadic);
- *self-relatedness of the body* – whether the body associates with itself, or [dissociates] itself from its corporeality.

It is as the body confronts these action problems that various types of body 'usage' emerge: disciplined, mirroring, dominating and communicative. Frank acknowledges that, empirically, bodies may not stay long with one type of usage. Instead, his objective is to provide a heuristic guide through which to understand behaviour (Frank 1991: 53).

In assessing both typologies, Shilling (1993) believes that whilst useful, they do not adequately explain 'why people should choose to adopt particular relations to their bodies, how individuals are able to change between styles of body usage, or what wider historical conditions could influence their adoption of certain styles rather than others'. Shilling feels that similar criticisms can be made of both approaches to the problem of the body. In particular, both are felt to adopt a 'core problems' approach which, he argues, is functionalist in essence. The only difference between the two typo-logies is the different levels at which such problems are addressed (society and individual). In sum, Shilling (1993) argues that they are not able ad-equately to conceptualize human agency. Turner is, in this sense, arraigned with Foucault and Douglas in seeing the body as significant only in relation to society. Frank, by contrast, whilst orienting the body's tasks to their social contexts, does accept the body as a corporeal phenomenon in his typology. The only difference between them is the different levels at which such problems are addressed, that is, society or individual: agency is effect-ively ignored.

Relatedly, Mary Douglas (1982, 1988) has delineated two bodies, the symbolic social body and the physical body. She has argued that we use the body's expressive resources to articulate symbolic and dichotomistic systems, and her work has been seminal in its influence in the social sciences. In her delineation of the 'two bodies' Douglas uses the techniques of structural analysis devised by Lévi-Strauss. For him, structural analysis is a process of sorting out basic oppositions that underlie complex cultural phenomenon (Lévi-Strauss 1981). This process shows the ways in which the phenomena being analysed and interpreted are both an expression of those contrasts and a reworking of them, thereby producing a culturally meaningful state-ment of order. In talking of the two bodies (the social and the physical body) she goes on to say that in the ongoing exchange of meanings the physical body is a very restricted medium of expression (Douglas 1982). Rather, symbols get their meaning from social experience and it is in this context that the body's expressive resources are used to articulate symbolic systems. The physical body is thus constrained by the social body; social forms are needed to impose bodily control.

Douglas later refined her position because of concern that it would be taken to mean that the physical body was simply Descartes' 'earthen machine' with no violation of its own. She gives the example of laughter, 'a unique bodily eruption which is always taken to be communication' (Douglas 1975) and which cannot be screened off, but which is incorpor-ated into discourse.

Similarly, these symbolic systems are not fixed. The margins between such classificatory systems – for example, pollution, or the preparation and consumption of meat – are in flux. This makes them vulnerable and demands management of these 'boundaries' through taboos and norms for behaviour and action. These semantic and social structures, particularly as pertain to bodily experiences, are a primary means through which experience is 'organized' or 'ordered' in culture. This common ground manifests itself in the cognitive structures and material actions of the social self. Turner (1980) has suggested that it is this, realized on the surfaces of bodies – decorated, clothed, shaped – in interaction with other bodies, that becomes the 'social skin', the boundary between social classes.

Douglas's general approach to body symbolism has been influential, particularly within the development of an anthropology of the body. The focus of a series of papers edited by Blacking (1977) was stated to be 'the cultural processes and products that are externalisations and extensions of the body in varying contexts of social interaction'. From this, the task of an anthropology of the body would be to 'experience others' bodies through our own bodies and to learn more of the somatic states that we can understand but about which little is known' (Blacking 1977: 6). In exploring premises for an anthropology of the body, Blacking drew upon Durkheim's notion of society as a system of active forces to argue that in the possibility of shared somatic states one finds the development of cultural forms (Blacking 1977: 11). From this he argued that, as extensions of capabilities that are already in the body, human behaviour and action can be seen in this context.

Elsewhere, Scheper-Hughes and Lock (1987) have attempted to integrate aspects of anthropological discourse around the body into work in the field of medical anthropology. In particular, drawing upon Mary Douglas, they state: 'We will begin from an assumption of the body as simultaneously a physical and symbolic artefact, as both naturally and culturally produced, and as securely anchored in a particular historical moment'. From this they move on to define the 'three bodies' discussed at the start of this chapter: a phenomenally experienced individual body-self; a social body; and a body politic, an 'artefact of social and political control' (Scheper-Hughes and Lock 1987: 6). They then propose that emotions may provide the medium of exchange and integration between these 'three bodies' in so far as 'emotions entail both feelings and cognitive orientations, public morality, and cultural ideology' (Scheper-Hughes and Lock 1987: 28). The focus on emotions as providing a critical juncture between individual and social modes of experience has also been pursued by Freund (1990) and Hochschild (1983).

The mapping of the body as a domain for anthropological (and specifically medical anthropological) enquiry remains consistent with the asymmetrical assumption of the social body constraining the phenomenally experienced individual body-self which underpins the approach of Douglas and, before her, of Durkheim. The individual body is, in this sense, no more than the immediate terrain for the ebb and flow of social forces. Similarly, Crawford (1984: 62) started from the idea that we live in a nature/culture opposition in which 'bodily experience is structured through the symbolic category of health'.

In sum, neither Frank nor Turner sufficiently conceptualizes human agency (Shilling 1993: 98). Turner is, in this sense, aligned with Foucault and Douglas, seeing the body as significant only in relation to society, whilst Frank, although orientating the body's tasks to their social contexts, does accept the body as a corporeal phenomenon in his typology.

In a similar way, the rise of second-wave feminism in the 1960s and 1970s led to a discounting of the body with the emphasis squarely on sexual politics (Kappeler 1994/95). The term 'gender' was adopted to enable the identification of masculinity and femininity as socially constructed roles in contrast to the notion of the female and male body (Oakley 1972). Sexual inequality, it was argued, could be removed by the restructuring of society to displace the oppression of women. The body was seen as the defining, naming characteristic of women used to justify treating women as the 'weaker sex'. So Phillips (cited in Cockburn 1991: 161) writes:

> Once feminists admit the mildest degree of sexual difference they open up a gap through which the currents of reaction will flow. Once let slip that premenstrual tension interfered with concentration, that pregnancy can be exhausting, that motherhood is absorbing, and you are off down the slope to separate spheres.

Under the influence of Foucault, postmodernism and poststructuralism, this line of thinking has, in recent years, given way to a philosophy in part based on difference; though this should not be seen as grounds for differential treatment (Shakespeare 1998). Women are not seen as either purely socially constructed or as a product of biological essentialism (Annandale and Clarke 1996). Strong social constructionist accounts of the gendered body fail to take account of the lived experiences of female and male bodies.

Feminists who espouse the 'difference' philosophy recognize the importance of the body in adequately explaining women's experience, but argue that it should not be seen as the basis of theory. Thus,

> [t]he body is not real or essential, we will not find all the answers that we seek within it. However, feminism cannot dispose of the body any more than it can simply inhabit it. The difference of bodies remains a fact – a fact that menaces instead of legitimating our understanding of sexual difference.
>
> (Elam 1994: 61)

This approach allows feminists to acknowledge the relationship between bodily processes and social relations. Shirley Prendegast's (1992) work on the experience of menarche and menstruation in schools is a good example of this. In contrast to the approach taken by many sociologists of the body, she actually talked to young women and found that the biological processes of puberty were mediated within specific social environments and, in the context of gender and power, with oppressive outcomes. Thus she manages to take account of biology, without reducing social and personal experiences to biology. Physiological reality is not dismissed, it is reworked. The political engagement and the materially grounded nature of such approaches to the body have resulted in a far more useful theoretical framework on the body than that available within sociology of the body itself (Shakespeare and Watson 1995).

Undeniably then, the emphasis placed on cultural and social concerns in much of the theorizing about the body, following the work of Douglas and under the influence of Foucault and second-wave feminism, has led to abstraction and generalization. The individual has been bracketed with little or no power of resistance to dominant ideologies. By expounding over-deterministic theories, sociology of the body appears to have ignored individuals as a creative force in determining their own lives; a point which, to be fair, Foucault began to recognize in his later work on technologies of the self (Foucault 1988).

Finally, the literature on the body is still largely void of the practical experiences of embodiment, with some exception in work on chronic illness (for example, Zola 1982; Murphy 1987; Kelly 1992). Little attempt has been made to present what Connell (1987: 83) has called the 'body as used or the body-I-am'. There are interesting things happening to people and their bodies which sociology of the body, relying as it does on a predominantly theoretical knowledge, has appeared unable or unwilling to investigate. Although in the sociology of health and illness the exploration of health through lay perspectives has been addressed (see, for example, Cornwell 1984; Backett 1992a, 1992b; MacInnes and Milburn 1994), we would argue that sociology of the body has yet to come to terms with lay understandings of the body or embodied experience. Frank (1991) called for theorizing to start from the body up. In this respect, the abstract claims of sociology of the body may, or may not, become more corporeal if they are grounded in the lived experiences of 'real people' as opposed to those of absent theorists.

This point has been recognized and argued by others, most notably Freund (1982, 1988, 1990). In identifying some features of 'human bodyliness', Freund (1990: 457) asserted that the embodied self is 'intimately meshed with social life' and that one consequence is that bodies should be studied as 'living, acting entities'. Crucially, in this respect, he made the case for the need to access lay perspectives, particularly in going on to argue that '[i]t is at the point of personal biography ... that exchanges between social life and a 'dynamic unconscious' take place and hence the point where mind, body and society meet' (Freund 1990: 471).

It is not argued that sociology of the body should pursue a purely empiricist enterprise. One can broadly agree with the agenda set out by Featherstone and Turner (1995) which identifies a number of major theoretical problems which require attention. Similarly, Frank's (1995: 187) assertion that even empirical enquiries must 'grapple with theoretical issues' should be considered. In this respect I and others have previously argued that the inter-relationship between culture, structure, behaviour and identity lies at the centre of the lived experience of 'the body', health and illness (Watson et al. 1996). A problem for theorizing the body is, in this instance, to make coherent sense of this articulation. This implies a need to focus on lived experience. In other words, lay accounts hold the conceptual keys to understanding the complex relationship between body, self, culture and society.

Summary

This chapter has attempted to demonstrate that contemporary treatment of the body has: mainly been theoretical rather than empirical; focused on the social body rather than the physical body; and tended to interpret the body from an etic (outsider/social science) perspective rather than from an emic (insider/lay) perspective. By contrast, female embodiment has, to an extent, been reclaimed and reassessed in the context of lay experience. However, critical consideration of the relationship between 'male' embodiment and health has not been a significant feature of the literature reviewed in the course of writing this book. Male embodiment, in this respect, remains largely 'unproblematic'; to adapt Lawler (1991), 'the [male] body has a fragmented, silent, and ambiguous presence'.

Note

1 This critique was originally developed for a doctoral thesis by the author. It was subsequently refined and presented at the 1995 BSA Medical Sociology Group Conference by the author in collaboration with S. Cunningham-Burley and N. Watson.

CHAPTER 3

THE CONTRIBUTION
OF LAY KNOWLEDGE

In the everyday lives of most people, health is not privileged – other meanings also shape a person's experience of their world, the social values they hold, the personal worth that they feel. Lupton (1994: 117) writes:

> It should be recognised that health-maintaining practices do not stand alone and above other practices of everyday life, but are incorporated seamlessly into the life-world of the individual, often in ways that submerge any overt 'health' associations under other meanings deemed to be more important to the individual's identity.

Thus, if the social-structural critique of the biomedical model (see Chapter 1) is to be taken seriously then we also need to deal with where it leads us. It could be argued that it leads us to confront macro-issues such as gender, race and class. Certainly, academics and practitioners have an understanding of the constraints within which people operate; but people may articulate such things differently. Wight (1993: 7) puts a very good case for our need to understand that lay perceptions and priorities may be expressed in other, more immediate ways:

> it is striking that the things which most concern people in Cauldmoss on a daily basis were, in terms of mainstream sociological theory, generally considered trivia . . . for instance the cleanliness of children's clothes, the relative expense of wedding presents, or personal reputation in the village. This was the stuff of status distinctions. Factors

deemed to be of sociological importance . . . occupation, class, voting behaviour, were usually experienced by villagers as the inevitable parameters of their condition, and therefore rather futile to dwell on. Within these bounds they led their lives, exercised by issues that were subject to their influence.

The significance of lay knowledge for public health

The extent to which this or that study provides a valid description or explanation of the social world of those subjects who provide researchers with 'their' data is a question that confronts all social scientists regardless of their methodological orientation. In public health, Chapman (1993) has most eloquently advanced this view. He says of the scientific tradition that it assumes a reductionist form of knowledge in which the gestalt of how various cultural, economic, organizational and educational factors combine to influence smoking behaviour is viewed as messy and unscientific. This messy gestalt is entangled in the explanatory gossamer of a myriad of experiences, conversations, memories, and exposures to interventions. Researchers bearing reductionist precepts and methods, he said, wore the equivalent of boxing gloves in their attempt to unravel these delicate threads. Chapman was making an important point: research to inform and assess public health measures needed to account for such complexity.

Relatedly, a meeting of public health 'experts' in Leeds in 1993 stated that in unravelling the complexities of the new public health there was a need to reformulate the scientific base, policy and practice of public health (Long 1993: 1). The fundamental question was 'the adequacy of current theory to support public health practice' (Long 1993: 2). Problems were identified with the nature and focus of epidemiological knowledge if progress was to be made in developing a more sophisticated understanding of how change for health gain at individual and community levels could be effected. In particular, it was noted:

> The underlying paradigm is clinical, leading to biomedical reductionism and associated victim blaming – causes of ill-health being seen as lying with individuals. There is a lack of serious attention to the social patterning of illness and the political and cultural influences on health.
> (Long 1993: 2)

The consensus that emerged from the discussion was that a response to this problem should include: extending the underlying paradigm from the individual to the community, organization and socioeconomic system; broadening methods to include and acknowledge the legitimacy of qualitative and participatory methods; and 'giving primacy to lay knowledge and beliefs' (Long 1993: 3).

This call to reformulate public health revolves around the relative contributions of scientific and lay knowledge to develop and assess the impact of interventions intended to improve health at all levels in society. This development is itself not accidental. It is bound up in and resonates with the broader social transformations currently shaping the *fin de siècle*: 'demographic factors such as the greying of populations . . . the changing nature of the disease burden [in developed countries] . . . the rise of consumer culture . . . the advent of new technologies' (Nettleton and Watson 1998a: 4–7) and, most singularly, the transition from the universal givens of modernity to the uncertainty of *late* or *high modernity* (Giddens 1991; Beck 1992). For example, Alasuutari (1992) argues that in the postmodern world existing explanatory models of alcoholism are not believed by modern individuals and individual alcoholics. In this context, contemporary therapies such as Alcoholics Anonymous are little more than stories with neat endings in which the problem is solved or disappears. Such stories are seen by Alasuutari to be losing authenticity as an effective recourse. This may be because, as Shilling (1993) argues, 'in high modernity, people have become unusually aware of their own unfinishedness'. Thus such therapies seem unrealistic, too finished to have meaning in the ebb and flow of everyday life. Shilling sees the consequence of this 'cynicism' as being a retreat from world-building activity. Alternatively, this could be seen as a different form of engagement with the world, one in which currency is given to change and adaptability (as presented by Martin 1994), in which explanation and interpretation are historically and socially contingent. Williams and Calnan (1996: 1613) have argued that life in late modernity is more *open*, and that our references for social life become more 'pluralized [with a] diversity of authorities and expertize'.

It is in this context that Byron Good provides a cautionary note. A medical anthropologist, Good was invited in 1990 to give the Morgan Lecture series at the University of Rochester, New York. The first of these focused on medical anthropology and the problem of belief. One of the first questions that Good posed was how the use of 'belief' is related to the epistemological assumptions of anthropologists. His preliminary assessment was that the term 'belief' was used in a way that signified error or falsehood, though such a position was seldom stated explicitly (Good 1994: 17). Good reviewed a number of anthropological texts and then proposed five hypotheses to account for the use of the concept of belief:

- The juxtaposition of 'belief' and 'knowledge' and the use of the term 'belief' to denote (or at least connote) counter-factual assertions. This despite a key goal of anthropology being to 'make understandable other societies in a non-judgemental way'.
- Belief as an analytical category in anthropology appeared to be most closely associated with religion and with discussions of folk-sciences.

That is, 'belief' was used particularly in cultural accounts of the unknown or in mistaken accounts of the 'natural world' where science could distinguish knowledge from belief.

- The term 'belief' appeared with varied frequency and analytical meaning in different theoretical paradigms. For example, it was less used in American anthropology, grounded in German historicist theorizing, but more prevalent in British social anthropology, especially in rationalist writing.
- The representation of others' culture as 'beliefs' authorized the position and knowledge of the observer.
- The term 'belief' continues to be an important odd-job word within the cognitive sciences and the medical social sciences where conflict between historicist interpretations (that any aspect of social life can only be understood in the context of the historical period in which it exists) and the claims of the natural sciences is most intense (Good 1994: 20–1).

In this sense, the analysis of culture as belief is said to reflect and reproduce an underlying epistemology and a particular structure of power relations (Good 1994: 20–1). As has been discussed earlier in this chapter, the authority of biomedical knowledge is being challenged but, as Good points out, one might also subject alternative social forms of knowledge to scrutiny. In this context, the language of the Leeds Declaration, for example, is interesting because, although it talks about the need to give 'primacy to lay knowledge and beliefs', it is ambiguous both about the status of lay knowledge *and beliefs* compared to scientific knowledge and the use of such knowledge in informing agendas for action to improve health.

It is particularly around the issue of risk assessment and management in public health that scientific (professional/research) and social (lay) knowledge pivots. Screening for risk factors of disease such as coronary heart disease has been and will continue to be a major activity in primary care (National Audit Office 1989; SODoH, PHPU 1996). At an individual level it is argued that primary health care professionals are well placed to give opportunistic preventive advice (Williams 1987; Cummings *et al.* 1989; Standing Medical Advisory Committee 1990). The focus in screening is upon those risk factors for which a scientifically valid causal link has been established (such as smoking and lung cancer). Ideally, the subsequent intervention will seek to identify and modify elevated risk factors by influencing the cognitive concerns of patients – attitudes, beliefs and motivations – in such a way that they adopt one or more of a range of medically approved behaviours.

Certainly, doctor- and nurse-led risk factor assessment and interventions can lead to modest risk factor changes that are significant for those at highest risk (Ashenden *et al.* 1997). But there is a problem. Many of those at higher risk, especially the socioeconomically disadvantaged, are less likely to respond to invitations for risk factor assessment. Rogers *et al.* (1997), drawing upon qualitative research into lay health beliefs and health inequalities, found significant differences in professional and lay views of health and behaviour, especially around the assessment of risk. Sometimes, no action or a different action to that proposed by a health professional was seen as the most rational action by a lay person. In some situations fatalism, *pace* Giddens (1991: 112), was better construed as a realistic appraisal of the potential for individual control over lifestyle choices. Behaviours viewed by some health professionals as negative (smoking, drinking) were seen by some as pleasurable parts of everyday life and essential to maintaining a sense of well-being and control (Davison *et al.* 1992). In contrast, some behaviours labelled as positive in public health discourse could be seen as detrimental to health. It has been argued that this standoff could be resolved by working 'with rather than against popular culture' (Backett and Davison 1992: 55). They asked for more understanding of commonly held ideas about the social and cultural contexts of health as a basis upon which to develop and implement initiatives to improve health. As such, professional and scientific explanations in isolation have their limitations (Williams and Calnan 1996). Arguably, the dialectic between scientific and lay (or social) knowledge should be based upon constructive engagement rather than ridicule (Pill and Stott 1987; Good 1994; Popay and Williams 1996). Both scientific and lay knowledge need to be used appropriately in the development and evaluation of policy, programmes and projects.

One of the most critical contributions that lay knowledge makes to policy and practice is that it can illuminate the interplay between structure and agency in people's daily lives. This is important for two reasons. First, it indicates something of the contested nature and capacity for change, at an individual level, of actions intended to improve health. Second, it introduces the concept of 'agency' into policy and practice considerations. Some of the most recent thinking in this area has been undertaken in the context of the UK Economic and Social Research Council's programme on social inequalities in health. Popay *et al.* (1998) argue that current theory and research on health inequalities (and, by implication, policy and practice) are limited because they do not readily address the relationship between structure and agency and, in particular, the possibility for and determinants of creative human agency. Between individuals and their capacity to act, they identify a number of 'mediating concepts'. These include, autonomy, control and identity and 'the central role of narratives in the "construction" of self-identity' (Popay *et al.* 1998: 637). In particular, they cite the work of Somers (1994), who argues that the experience of social action is constituted through narratives (Popay *et al.* 1998: 638). They end by suggesting that in the context of health inequalities there is a 'strong case for looking at people's perceptions of "episodes" in their lives and the ways in which these may orientate or fail to orientate action at the individual or collective level' in the context of place and time (Popay *et al.* 1998: 639). The remainder of this chapter and Chapter 5 provide a bridge into a grounded analysis of informant accounts, which suggests that the primary 'place' from which we interact with the world around us is the body.

Lay concepts of health

In this section we start to open up a further perspective in our understanding of men's health by providing an overview of the concepts of health held by a group of men who guided me through the spaces and tensions, dramas and celebrations of their lives over a two-year period in the early 1990s.[1] For example, what did they mean when they talked about themselves or others 'being healthy' or 'unhealthy'? What factors did they associate with health or lack of health and how was this manifested?

Generally, the men in this study shared similar ideas concerning the definition of health. Health was usually felt to result from physical and mental actions which, in their turn, produced emotional well-being. The following statement was typical:

> If I adhere to a proper diet, take a reasonable amount of exercise and mentally stay attuned I feel good, and if I feel good I am happy with life.
>
> (Car salesman, 36)

Some accounts of health were just as likely to infer from a mental state that one is healthy:

> If you're happy and content it's a good sign that you're enjoying life to its full . . . you know . . . If you're happy you're usually healthy.
>
> (Communications supervisor, 33)

Health was also defined in terms of the need to meet certain obligations traditionally associated with masculinity:

> I need to be healthy to stay in a job. I need to be healthy to provide an income for my wife and family.
>
> (Software engineer, 34)

Without exception, informants saw health as an aspiration all too easily compromised. This was stated quite explicitly:

> I don't think anybody is 100 per cent healthy . . . there'll be something about everybody that'll prevent them being 100 per cent fit or 100 per cent healthy.
>
> (Electrician, 33)

According to informant accounts, that 'something' included the following: the pressure of work; 'difficulty in motivating yourself all the time'; social obligations; the body 'not being up to it any more'; being 'dependent' on your partner for what you eat; and 'not having the time'.

Informants' definitions of health were essentially pragmatic and grounded in the need to fulfil everyday gendered obligations. These definitions of health covered physical, mental, emotional and social features. Further analyses of the interview transcripts revealed that these features were present in six main ways, although ideas did tend to overlap and were presented as groupings of elements, not simply as discrete entities. The six ways in which informants thought about health were as: a resource to live and work with; physical and, to a lesser extent, mental fitness; a sense of emotional, mental and/or physical well-being; physical appearance; absence of disease or illness; and the product of, or signified by, one or more health-related behaviours.

Health as a resource

Health was frequently conceptualized as a resource that enabled a person to live and work productively. Elsewhere, Herzlich (1973) identified the concept of health as a reserve enabling the individual to overcome adversity and maintain good health. Williams (1990) found a similar concept among older Aberdonians. In this sense, it meant being able to maintain health despite some debilitating illness or condition. In the context of the current study, health as a resource meant being able to deal with situations and obligations which informants faced on a day-to-day basis. One informant, dealing with the maintenance of heavy plant equipment, said:

> Obviously, if I'm not in good health I wouldn't be able to work where I work.
>
> (Mechanic, 39)

A builder who owned his own company put it similarly:

> if I get up in the morning, go away to my work, come home at a reasonable time, not too late because I am a bit of a workaholic sometimes . . . then I am healthy.
>
> (Builder, 33)

This notion of health as a resource was one that most informants mentioned whatever their socioeconomic status. Having this resource enabled social obligations, primarily to family, to be met:

> Being able to get up in the morning. Do the job I am meant to do. Have time for my children, have time for my wife, and basically get on with day to day living.
>
> (Warehouse manager, 35)

This last informant cites specific obligations that he needs to fulfil. Kristiansen (1989) explored the meanings attached to health in a British sample of men and women. She found that among men, health was associated with 'family security', whereas women associated health with 'happiness', a comfortable life' and 'pleasure' (Kristiansen 1989: 187). In other words, the men in her sample perceived health within the context of values, which could be construed as relevant to a concern with the welfare of others. Relatedly, a later study found that the best univariate predictors of men's well-being were perceived closeness to partner, adjustment to the husband role and number of close friends (Julian *et al.* 1992).

Crawford (1984) has argued that in the public world of production and the marketplace, people are under a moral obligation to maintain health in order to work. Few of those respondents who expressed this notion had strong religious beliefs or active practices, which suggests that the sense of obligation implicit in these accounts is a secularized version of the Protestant work ethic that Williams (1990) found informed the attitudes towards health and illness of older Aberdonians. A general feeling was that 'if I'm not in good health I wouldn't be able to work' and that 'I have to be able to work to earn money'. Informants in both the current study and that reported by Williams appear, in this sense, to be proffering definitions of the male role, in this instance as a family 'provider' through the ability to get and retain a job.

Health as fitness

Most informants talked of health as fitness at some point in the first interview and often returned to it in subsequent interviews. It was also clear that health as a resource and health as fitness were closely related in informant accounts. Fitness both enabled and was the product of activity, whether that activity be exercise or work:

> The type of work I have chosen involves physical work so my muscles have to be able to handle it.

> (Derrick hand, 35)

Similarly:

> I've never had a problem with walking, climbing and stuff like that. I mean just . . . physical exercise, at work, you know what I mean. That's why I suppose I'm fit.

> (Mechanical engineer, 40)

Fitness was relevant since it allowed one to 'cope better' with everyday life. Being fit was sometimes implied through an absence of signs of being unfit, – although inappropriate or unexpected exertion could lead to 'being out of breath', 'out of puff' or 'flabbered'. This relates to a commonsensical notion that men are often 'blind' to their own physical shortcomings. However, some informants were sensitive to potential impact of signals of inactivity:

I seem to have developed a spare tyre . . . It doesn't look good and it can't be doing me any good either.

(HGV driver, 31)

Informants who talked of health as being fit did not generally assess their level of fitness in terms of levels of activity as recommended by health professionals (at least three periods of strenuous physical exercise every week, each period lasting at least 20 minutes). Rather, they relied on alternative standards. Some informants looked to their own past for comparison, that is, 'feeling as fit as you did when you were younger'. A prevalent standard among those informants who generally took no hard physical exercise was that a good level of fitness was having 'sufficient' fitness. This was judged as being able to comfortably do what you need to do, as being 'fit to do what you want to do':

Even going for a walk is exercise as far as I'm concerned. As long as I can get from A to B and feel reasonably fit doing it. If I thought I needed more then I would do it.

(Teacher, 40)

For others, the level of sufficiency was stated more precisely as being related to the ability to undertake specific tasks:

Fitness is for a purpose. If the purpose is to walk everywhere then you should be fit enough to cope with that. Being healthy is just being fit enough to get by.

(Technician, 32)

Even among those taking occasional exercise, fitness was something that they did at their own pace, at a 'level I feel comfortable with'. The notion of having just enough fitness was also mentioned by informants who took more regular exercise. One informant, who is a member of a local football team, training once a week, and who also plays golf, said:

I can work pretty hard if I have to and it doesn't affect me much. Compared to younger lads or older blokes who pick up something or walk a mile and end up in a sweat . . . knackered . . . I think I'm reasonably fit in that context.

(Engineer, 39)

It is interesting to note that only two of the informants who smoked were currently taking part in sports activity (football) on a regular basis. For them, as for smokers who used to exercise regularly, there seemed to be no contradiction between being fit and being a smoker. One informant, now a diabetic, when in the Army used to take part in cross-country running on a competitive basis. He said:

Well, there was a team of five of us and two of us smoked and we figured that because we kept on training, kept on running, that our lungs must be twice the size of guys who didn't smoke. Because we were having to inhale just as much air and work just as hard, so we must be more fit than the others. We had a joke about that, but we did go . . . on a cross-country championship run and actually stopped and sat on a rock and still made the winning team. I think that as long as you keep fit at that level of keeping fit I don't think it matters if you smoke that much. You are clearing yourself out. It is probably just the long-term effects that you will start to notice later on.

(Technical design manager, 37)

His rationale was that the level of activity was sufficient to overcome or compensate for the 'clogging-up of the gunge' in his lungs. The notion that being fit by taking part in sports conferred health benefits whilst delaying the negative effects of smoking was similar to one held by non-smoking sports participants who felt that current fitness might be achieved to the detriment of some future impact on the body such as cartilage trouble.

Fitness was also seen as an indicator of how efficient one's body was – efficient in the sense of being able to perform work or leisure tasks without undue discomfort:

Being active, being fit. Not suffering from any illnesses . . . not having any barriers preventing you doing anything.

(Catering supervisor, 32)

Equally, fitness had mental dimensions:

If you don't feel fit and healthy you won't think fit and healthy . . . If the body is tired and overweight, if your body is not fit then your mind is not fit.

(Unemployed roustabout, 39)

Corresponding with Saltonstall's (1993) findings, informants tended to indicate that fitness was generally seen as deriving from work, sports activity such as football, or outdoor activity such as hill walking, and less from indoor exercise such as working out or keep-fit.

What is striking about the ways in which informants talked of 'being fit' is the possibility that, as used by the men in this study, fitness may have a significance beyond the rather narrow medical or health educator's concept of physical and (to a lesser extent) mental fitness. That is, fitness as a concept has a social dimension by which the men in this study measure their ability to undertake the social obligations to work, partner, family, friends and community that are made explicit in the ways in which they articulated 'male' roles earlier in this chapter.

Blaxter (1990) found that 'fit' was the most common word used by men aged under 40 to describe their health. Being fit, both mentally and physically, was the most salient and clearly articulated manifestation of health for informants irrespective of occupational status. Mullen (1992) has also found the salience of notions of fitness to health among manual and non-manual workers. By contrast, d'Houtaud and Field (1984) concluded that fitness derived from exercise was associated with non-manual workers, whereas fitness derived from activity such as work was a notion prevailing among manual workers. Bourdieu has also argued that bodies and the way we use them – the deployment of physical capital (Bourdieu 1978) – is class-based in so far as '[t]he cognitive structures which social agents implement in their practical knowledge of the social world are internalized, "embodied" social structures' (Bourdieu 1984). Fundamental to this is Bourdieu's notion of 'habitus' – that an individual internalizes as natural the tastes of his class. The body is the foundation of these tastes. In the 'working classes' the body is instrumental. It is employed as a 'means to an end' – to work, to provide. Then, as one moves up the class hierarchy, the body is treated as 'an end in itself'. Differences in findings between studies based on French and Scottish samples may be accounted for by cultural differences in how health is conceptualized – in the case of the Scottish, by the impact of a work ethic across classes, originally using religion as the means of diffusion. Equally, there may be no tension in the two sets of findings, in that the Glasgow study (Mullen 1992) and the French study may contain a preponderance of informants from working-class backgrounds.

Health as well-being

That accounts of well-being tended to be grounded in embodied experience is apparent from informant accounts. Among those respondents who did not take much exercise this sense of embodied well-being was fairly passive, that is, functional:

> Health is an overall state of well-being, or a measure of well-being and that can be everything from your organs functioning correctly right up to your brain functioning correctly.
>
> (Technical design manager, 37)

Among those few respondents who took regular exercise this sense of well-being was more vivid and active:

> You don't have nae aches or nagging feelings or undercurrents of pain anywhere within your body . . . I like the feeling you get if you have maybe jogged five or six miles. The blood starts to tingle all through the muscles. To me, I feel best when I feel like that. That is why I keep active. If I am gardening I tend to dig for no reason other than I like the exercise on your shoulders. I like jogging and . . . running round the squash court. I like the tingle you get afterwards. Your skin sort of glows and you feel good.
>
> (Industrial chemist, 38)

However, for some respondents, physical well-being was linked to mental well-being, though this was sometimes expressed in a fairly general way.

Just the general feeling of wellbeing within yourself, your body.

(Safety engineer, 31)

Being healthy means feeling good.

(Mechanical engineer, 37)

Others expressed this association more directly:

If you are not physically up to it, it must have an effect on you mentally.

(Safety engineer, 31)

Looked at from another angle, lack of mental 'fitness' may inhibit physical fitness:

without feeling mentally fit I don't think that you can do so much about your physical fitness because you are not in the right frame of mind.

(Electrician, 34)

the physical side is . . . keeping in shape in terms of having enough energy to do things. The energy also, I think, is affected by your mental health.

(Quantity surveyor, 37)

However, this linking of the physical and the mental as a definition of well-being was not shared by all respondents, with some arguing that

if you're happy with the way you feel then I suppose it's a case you think you're healthy.

(Drilling equipment salesman, 38)

For these respondents, well-being was a state of mind. In some respects this viewpoint was tinged with uncertainty as to how one can determine mental well-being.

I think the mental side would probably be the more critical side . . . we don't know what our physical or mental limitations are, but physically you can visualize things and you see what you classify as fitness and . . . not fit. But mentally you don't see that. It is very difficult to perceive who is mentally healthy and who is not, so I would be more worried about the mental side . . . the mental side would have to be the one you have to get right or be reasonably right before you could be sure of the physical side.

(Safety engineer, 31)

The notion of an embodied well-being refers to the groundedness of our sense of self and our experience of the world, in the body. Elias (1978) has argued that one cannot separate out the psychological, sociological and physical elements of being human because historically they have developed together. Similarly, Illich (1986) has come to the view that the Western body should be seen as a progressive embodiment of self.

Health as physical appearance

Health as physical appearance appears to be linked to health as well-being, particularly in the sense of 'performance' and how others perceive that 'performance'. Generally, comment about health as appearance would be made by the informant about others:

> I have actually got a guy who stays two doors down from us. You should see him, he is incredible. Ever see the magazine *Viz* . . . there was two lassies in there and they were called the 'fat slags' and they were really unhealthy and this guy . . . walks about and the stomach hangs over his trousers.
>
> (Builder, 33)

Equally, some informants had been the target of such comment. The unemployed roustabout, who smokes and doesn't feel that his diet is very healthy, said:

> I have come out of the shower and there are six guys in your room and they say 'you better lose some weight you fat bastard or you will be dead in a couple of years time.'
>
> (Unemployed roustabout, 39)

Another informant who feels he gets taunted at work because of his weight, which he attributes to his 'build', but who used to play football, take part in competitive canoeing and go hill walking was very conscious of the response his appearance might provoke:

> going out, not feeling conscious about someone looking at you thinking 'God, he is fat'. Being able to run about with the kids. Not sitting pecking all the time, general health. Just feeling healthy.
>
> (Garage service manager, 32)

Some respondents linked this sense of health as appearance to notions of fitness. But as with fitness, any sense of what might be appropriate for the respondent is retrospective, referring to their own past.

> You know you are overweight. I know the way it used to be. I know I was never overweight and I was always very fit and what I am finding now is that I am overweight and have lost my fitness.
>
> (Teacher, 40)

Health as absence of disease or illness

Not suffering from a particular disease, illness or other condition or disability was cited by many respondents as evidence of 'having' health. This concept of 'having' or 'not having' health, illness or disability suggests that health may be perceived as a possession – that the individual 'owns' their condition, whatever it may be. This resonates with the earlier concept of health as a resource, as something personal, held by or residing within the person. Thus, one informant, a smoker, when asked what health was, said:

> Just being well . . . not having any disability that prevents you doing what you enjoy.
>
> (Training consultant, 40)

This idea of 'having' or 'owning' what one experiences is primarily located in the body. Hence, another informant who plays football in a local league said health was:

> Not feeling I've got a sore bit here or I am all choked up and just being able to get up, no sore bits, no aches and pains.
>
> (Electrician, 34)

What these two examples also show is that whereas health facilitates social action, illness, disability or other minor complaints can prevent an informant fulfilling obligations, whether to work, to the family, to the sports team, or to 'doing what you enjoy'. In consequence, one might argue that the concept of having personal health would fit comfortably with the promotion of the concept of individual responsibility for health.

However, having health or having it taken away, for example, by 'taking a heart attack' (an interesting notion that may suggest that a reciprocal exchange occurs) is often felt to be governed by chance, luck or fate (Davison *et al.* 1992). Even an informant who exercises regularly and consciously eats a healthy diet could comment that 'I have been lucky, I am rarely ill'. Another, who also feels that he follows a healthy lifestyle, said:

> Having said all that, there's all these other things that can happen. You know, the worst types of illness. The cancers and these sorts of things which can happen to you regardless of . . . how you live your life.
>
> (Engineer, 38)

A note on health as behaviour(s)

Studies usually report a further way in which health is conceptualized – as health-related behaviour (Blaxter 1990; Mullen 1993; MacInnes and Milburn 1994). Reference to health as health-related behaviour permeated all informant accounts. Eating, drinking, exercise, smoking or not smoking, and relaxation were articulated as part and parcel of everyday living. This suggests that they are used as a common-sense reference for health in day-to-day discourse. However, in the sense in which they were referred to, health was the product of certain behaviours, which individually or collectively contributed to or militated against 'being healthy'. Thus, men's talk about health is contextualized within references to other aspects of everyday life deemed relevant. To this extent, the men in this study did not usually see health as a specific topic except where doing so moved it into the domain of professional discourse, for example 'going to the doctor'.

The body and health in lay accounts

What was particularly evident in informant accounts from the moment when analysis began was the presence – sometimes implied, at other times explicit – of the body. Thus, when respondents talked about health, particularly when conceptualized as a resource, as fitness, appearance or well-being, they implicitly or explicitly grounded their accounts in terms of their own or others' bodies. This may seem like common sense. What should one expect but that informants would talk about their bodies? However, it may also be indicative of the degree to which the body is taken for granted in male conceptualizations of health. At the time when fieldwork began, I was certainly uncritically wedded to the notion that men's health was largely a hormone-induced behavioural problem. The realization that a number of informants were spontaneously inserting this embodied dimension into their discourse on personal experience of health was gradually confirmed as the interviews progressed, and so lay theorizing about the lived body became a major focus for exploration and clarification.

Healthy images

The idea of the body as the primary location of health and the degree to which it operates in constructing self and others' health was explored by asking informants to describe people whom they saw as being healthy and unhealthy. Healthy people were described using a mixture of body image and health behaviours. For example:

> *Interviewee (I):* Well, just somebody who is the right weight for their height and keeps themselves, sort of tidy appearance and, ken, a bit of exercise.
> *Researcher (R):* When you say 'tidy appearance' what do you mean by that?
> *I:* Well, just sort of, usually someone who is into keep-fit. Is real slim and immaculate in their tracksuits and usually you can pick them out.
> (Mechanic, 39)

So, someone who is healthy is noticeable, almost packaged. They give the appearance of being in control. When describing someone who is healthy a few informants would use the example of a brother(-in-law) or father(-in-law). Speaking of his father, as several did, one informant said:

> He had an outdoor job, which was fairly physical. He ate nearly every vegetable that he grew himself organically. He used to cycle to work. Had plenty of exercise as well.
>
> (Garage service manager, 32)

Another informant, describing his brother as someone he saw as healthy, said:

> John would bike over by Durris, over Slug Road and back on Sundays . . . he doesn't smoke . . . he used to play football. Not now. He likes a lot of exercise. He doesn't eat junk food. So John, I would say, would be a clean living healthy person.
>
> (Builder, 33)

Whilst the first account explicates the body in terms of appearance, the next two focus on activity. In these the body has not materialized physically, but one might argue that such activity is projected from and concerned with the embodied individual. Further, such accounts of healthy people almost always defined the healthy other as of the same sex. In the last two cases respondents are describing someone known to them. Likewise in both, the image of the healthy person is fairly stylized, conforming in patterns of behaviour to those recommended by health professionals as being at the 'core' of a healthy lifestyle. This stylization of image is even more pronounced when the respondent found it difficult to think of a healthy person who was known to them. In such instances, the researcher was offered the following type of description – an idealized stereotype, not a living individual:

> He would be just the right weight for his height. He wouldn't smoke, or drink too much. He would have regular exercise, regular amounts of sleep as well as healthy food.
>
> (Mechanical engineer, 40)

In the three preceding accounts, the body-in-action as applied through exercise or some other physical activity emerges, together with health-related behaviours that tend the body, such as eating and sleeping or not smoking and drinking to excess. The preceding quotation is a good example of a dominant image in the study data of someone who is judged to be healthy. As a social construction it contains three main levels of description. First, it shows that the description of weight and height corresponds closely to clinical standards for ideal body mass ratios; another informant said a healthy person would be '5 foot 11 inches and 11 stone'. The second part of the quotation offers a list of behaviours that echoed contemporary medical and policy discourse regarding health promoting behaviours (Department of Health 1989; Scottish Office Home and Health Department 1991; Scottish Office Department of Health 1992). As to reasons for this congruence between lay and clinical knowledge a few informants did, over the course of the fieldwork, mention television programmes which had covered health issues, or reading stories in the press. A comment by one informant points to his wife's preoccupation with weight as having some bearing on this congruence:

> She is very pernickety with her weight, not so much fitness, but actually healthy weight. She is very into this height and weight. Ideal weight for your height, although she says she is a few pounds over weight.
>
> (Garage service manager, 32)

Since this line of questioning was not actively explored one can only speculate that exposure to debate, images and information about health through the mass media, and possibly partners, has produced such congruence between lay and clinical knowledge. Finally, both the above levels of description come together in a third. In this third level, informants make an assumption about the link between body shape and behaviours that are likely to have produced that configuration. All three levels combine to form a particular image of the body.

Unhealthy images

In this, as in other responses to the invitation to describe people whom they saw as being healthy, informants may have been furnishing socially acceptable public accounts of someone who is healthy (Cornwall 1984; Backett 1992a, 1992b). Further, this response could have been shaped by an informant's perception of who the researcher is – someone associated vaguely with their local health centre or, more frequently, a doctor. The evidence for this can be found, for example, in a few instances during the course of the fieldwork, when informants wanted the researcher to examine something that had been troubling them (particularly delicate and personal problems in one instance), or, when arriving at an informant's house the door would be opened by the informant or his partner with a shouted comment back into the house that 'the doctor's here!'. This despite having clearly identified myself before the start of the first interview as a researcher interested in what they believed and did about health and not a doctor.

The same sorts of description occurred again when informants were asked to describe someone who might be unhealthy. In describing unhealthy people, body image often predominated over signs of health behaviour. When the latter signs are given they are generally expressed as negative or unhealthy behaviours associated with eating, drinking and smoking. One would not necessarily expect this to be different if women were commenting about

other women (idealized or not). However, previous studies do suggest that
women have rather sophisticated concepts of health (Woods *et al.* 1988;
Martin 1989). Blaxter (1990), in analysing responses to a national health
and lifestyle survey, found that women gave more expansive answers than
most men. For example, very few men included social relationships in their
definitions of health or raised the concept of 'energy' and 'vitality' (Blaxter
1990: 30).

In the present study, though, informants found it easier to think of a
person known to them when asked to describe someone who is unhealthy.
In particular, work mates were often talked about in this context:

> Alcoholic work mates. You know, they're wrecked. Burst blood vessels,
> washed out, always sweating.
>
> (Electrician, 34)

As with images of the healthy person, descriptions could be quite stylized:

> Someone who leads an unhealthy lifestyle never ever considers exer-
> cise. Wouldn't think twice about taking the car one hundred yards up
> the road. Someone who drinks and eats to excess all the wrong foods
> . . . someone that is 5 feet 4 inches and 15 stone. Totally gross.
>
> (Warehouse dispatcher, 31)

Again, the researcher is offered a socially constructed description containing contemporary lifestyle messages regarding health behaviour, wrapped
up in a very powerful and value-laden body image. Perhaps this was nothing
more than a public account of an unhealthy person given to a researcher
often perceived as 'the doctor'? It is interesting that in such descriptions
– and the one that follows – height should figure so regularly and not
just references to 'fatness'. It may be that height has value as a cultural
marker of health and social status. Another consideration could be that
people do not realize that they now have a model and language for health
that they never had before. In this sense, in their accounts informants may
be articulating an approximate definition of (in)appropriate health-related
behaviours through the language and concepts that are available to them.

The image of the grossly overweight type of person tended to appear
in most accounts of unhealthy people. Interestingly, in contrast to descriptions of healthy people, informants were more prepared to furnish female
examples – colleagues at work, a woman they had noticed in the street, or
their partner – when describing someone who they felt was unhealthy. For
example, talking of a former colleague, a car salesman said:

> Probably a girl I used to work with in the last company. Very sad.
> She is still very young, about 22 or 23 . . . 5 foot 1 inch, about 18 or
> 19 stone. Doesn't take exercise at all. Sits at her desk all day. Her idea
> of an evening out is to get a video out . . . when she first joined the

company she was probably about 8 stone, very thin. She has actually got a twin sister . . . they were very similar, now they are like chalk and cheese. Yet her sister goes to aerobics and swimming and she does none of this.

(Car salesman, 36)

Taken together, these various levels of description combine to form symbolic shared images of generally, but not always, male bodies. The symbolic modalities by which the healthy and unhealthy are described conform in broad terms to psychological notions of desirable and undesirable male body forms: the endomorph (short and fat: 'slovenly'), the mesomorph (broad shoulders, narrow waist and hips: 'healthy') and the ectomorph (tall and thin: 'nervous'). A strand of psychological research over the past four decades has used mainly male college student samples to explore the desirability and role of body form. In particular, such research has investigated relationships between body form and behaviour (Brodsky 1954; Sugerman and Haronian 1964; Dibiase and Hjelle 1968; Mahoney 1974; Montemayor 1978; Mishkind *et al.* 1987).

Despite this image, some respondents did qualify the descriptions by suggesting that some people just could not help 'the way they were built'. This notion of the body as a resource, of being the way you are built, seems to ground health in a body that is received and largely immutable – an inherited body. This corresponds to Herzlich's (1973) notion of a 'reserve of health':

You can do all the healthy things you will but if you haven't got that healthy body at first then there is nothing you can do about it . . . You can improve things and lessen what you've got, but you've got what you've got.

(Quantity surveyor, 37)

Informants' ideas about having 'the body you're born with' – a natural quota of health – should be distinguished from the concept of physical capital as described by Bourdieu (1978, 1984) and Shilling (1991). In this latter concept, the body becomes the medium for the production, conversion and transmission of values (habitus and taste) that reflect its particular class position *vis-à-vis* other bodies (Shilling 1991: 654–5). Physical capital in these terms operates, in informant accounts, within the context of their descriptions of healthy and unhealthy others. We have already alluded to the possible importance of 'height' in such descriptions.

Thus, informants in this study and others (see, for example, Watson *et al.* 1996) acknowledged that symbolic representations of the body allowed the evaluation of others' health. However, it should not be assumed that the use of cultural ideals about healthy bodies in health promotion is either desirable or practicable. Caution should be exercised inasmuch as the images of healthy and unhealthy bodies that are made explicit in the context of public discourse on health do not easily translate into the everyday worlds of informants.

Bodily images in health advertising

I wanted to explore further how informants used the sorts of images which they had presented to me. What was to become clear was that informants used such symbolic representations of the male body to evaluate other men's health. Coincidentally, just before the final round of interviewing, a Department of Health advert depicting a well-muscled male in the pose of Rodin's *The Thinker* (Figure 3.1) appeared in newspapers and magazines across the United Kingdom. Referred to by the DoH Information Office as *Mechanical Man*, the advertisement was used to promote its *Health of the Nation* booklet (DoH 1992). The purpose of the advertisement was to prompt men to write in or ring for a copy of the booklet as the first step in taking responsibility for their own health. The metaphorical image alluded to in the advert was that the body is like a machine and that machines need looking after.

This advertisement was mentioned spontaneously by a few of the informants, and I showed it to those who did not mention it spontaneously because it provided a graphic illustration of body form associated with health that informants had spoken about in earlier interviews. Informants made some interesting comments that questioned the effectiveness of the particular stylized image of the 'perfect male body' and of the desirability and ability of developing and maintaining such a body image of masculinity in the context of everyday life. Participants were first asked to describe what they saw when shown the advert.

> Well, it's a man, physically fit, strong looking, big shoulders, muscles in the arms, well-shaped thighs . . . Also the stance – what muscle men do – not lying back all flabby and soft . . . It's not really me because it is much stronger physically . . . putting something out like that, it's the image of a goal which very few folk will achieve . . . I would never worry about not having a body like that.
>
> (Warehouse manager, 35)

The image was further criticized as an inappropriate cultural representation of the 'normal bloke's everyday body'. One which identified the body as a desirable object in the same way that advertisers use female body images which are aspirational stereotypes.

> It's a bit like having a female sitting here with a bikini, which is what the advertisers perceive as the perfect body.
>
> (Electrical maintenance co-ordinator, 37)

Figure 3.1 *Health of the Nation* advertisement, 1992

Gives me the impression of somebody who goes and pumps iron every day. It's the body beautiful who swanks along the side of the pool when he's on holiday. Expects everybody to admire his body.

(Quantity surveyor, 37)

A common response was that 'you are just the shape (or weight) you are'. Informants went further in objectifying the image presented to them. Indeed, the image was perceived by some respondents as having homoerotic associations. The individual in the advert being identified as 'a model', 'a poser' and 'a poof'. But criticism was not just confined to the appearance of the particular body in the advert. The meanings implicit in that body image for some respondents signified 'danger', 'fanaticism' and 'taking things to extremes', with no real certainty of healthy outcomes such as prolonged or improved quality of life. Respondents cited extreme forms of exercise. For example:

> You can't just stop [weightlifting] because your body, you know, it gets accustomed to it . . . and if it's not getting exercise all the time, your body's bound to go all to hell . . . you'll start putting on the flab.
>
> (Builder, 33)

> [Athletes] get to the stage where the body breaks down so quickly that, you know, they've got to top it up with all their pills . . . and then the body isn't healthy.
>
> (Technician, 32)

> Mates of mine . . . marathon runners . . . clock up to 100 miles a week, yet they would go to bed at eight . . . because they're so shattered and they would sleep during dinnertime at school. In my mind that's not a fit person. That's somebody who is ready to drop . . . it's artificial fitness.
>
> (Teacher, 39)

Even the pursuit of physical activity perceived to be less obsessional and more social, such as being a member of a local football team, was felt to be ultimately detrimental to the health of one's body:

> the legs are probably functioning better now, because of the sports activity but when I stop doing that [football] in years to come, it's highly probable I'll have, if I'm going to have arthritis, it's going to be in things like the knees and the ankles.
>
> (Electrician, 33)

Exercising to this degree at a professional level was understood to aid performance. However, achieving such performance goals may be seen to 'build in' or 'accelerate' future bodily fragmentation. Fitness acquired by professionals and other non-elite sportsmen and women is perceived by some informants who do not exercise regularly as being artificial. The body is a fragile artifice, manufactured through the application and repetition of rigorous training regimes. These regimes are perceived to be followed at the expense of everyday social obligations, particularly with regard to the family. In this sense informants' attitudes towards such individuals are not couched in terms of admiration, rather it is a 'detached' and somewhat critical commentary that they offer.

In a sense the body, thus articulated, could paradoxically be said to be distorting the physical/social body relationship by abstaining from the everyday social ordering of physical bodies which could act to marginalize the body. It was precisely this point that many of the informants who did not take regular exercise were reacting against in their comments about the DoH advertisement – that to achieve that body would require of them a selfish act of discipline to the detriment of desirable (and preferable?) obligations to family and work. One informant summed up his response – and the subverting influence of consumerism – when he said: 'It's either get your body back together or buy a new wardrobe' (Electrical maintenance co-ordinator, 37).

The advert also failed to convince these men to take action because the image of the male body offered to them (not a 'normal everyday body') obscured the health education message. This was that the body is like a machine and so needs looking after, a way of speaking about the body which the men in this study also used.

By contrast, Figure 3.2 shows an advertisement commissioned as part of a series for an Edinburgh health club. The advertising strategy ignored popular cultural notions of the body and looked for its icons to people who it might be said embody the tensions of daily living and resistance to cultural notions of an ideal body. Certainly the advertisement was responsible for a major increase in recruitment to that health club, and actually is a more accurate reflection of the types of people who attend the club that I have periodically dragged myself along to. In other words some informants argued that they have a 'natural' physical form. This echoes, in some respects, the idea that women have natural shapes that are distorted by patriarchal forces (Chernin 1983; Orbach 1988). Informant accounts would suggest that this constitutes almost a form of resistance to social pressure to adopt health-promoting behaviours or develop 'healthy bodies', a notion due to Crawford (1984).

'A real mess': weight and identity

Images of the bodybuilder and the marathon runner represent one end of a continuum of the appropriate relationship between body image, self-image and health behaviour. The opposite end of the continuum, around which are clustered male stereotypes such as 'the slob' and 'the couch potato', represents another extreme manifestation of the relationship between body image, self-image and health behaviour. At this latter extremity, loss of body shape or spoiled identity results from unhealthy behaviours, such as over-eating and sustained heavy consumption of alcohol, which 'break down' body image from within. The products of such behaviour reveal themselves in or map themselves on to the body.

Figure 3.2 Health club advertisement
Reproduced by permission: The Leith Agency, The Edinburgh Club and Victor Albrow

He would be eating thousands of calories a day and he had a huge stomach. He had a sagging chest and he had a pallor about him.

(Industrial chemist, 38)

Distorted body shapes can occur in two main ways. The first of these occurs as excess breaks down male body shape, altering posture, adding and redistributing fat so that a new body shape, as perceived by others, begins to emerge – a shape that parodies female body form.

He has a chest like a woman, his chest has obviously grown as well . . . in fact if he wore make-up he would look like a woman . . . if he dressed like one. Although this guy was only about 27 years old he was a mess.

(Mechanic, 39)

To talk of 'distorted shape' implies that there exists some conception of what is a normal male body shape. In talking of others, the conception of 'normal' shape would appear to be derived from the mesomorphic model, in the sense that it represents a cultural – and hence public – understanding of what is masculine. Looking older than you are, especially when talking of younger or same-age colleagues at work, represents the second and more common type of lost body shape. Here, the body's appearance is prematurely aged. For example, talking of life working offshore, informants would comment on how aspects of the lifestyle and the perception among some workers of the rigs being a 'man's world' led to 'excessive appetites'. One informant raised this subject when he was asked whether he felt that he and his wife had similar attitudes to health:

Just having a pair of balls is the whole difference . . . men work offshore – they have got to be strong and fit. Women couldn't do it anyways . . . they say that when they are out there. But when they come home they are drinking seven pints a day and they are smoking dope and doing all this and they are just physical wrecks . . . and they think they are fit because they work offshore . . . The day you are coming off you say to someone . . . 'Well you will be blootered tonight then will you? Which pub do you drink in?' It's as if everybody has to do it, and half of them do it because the other half say they do it . . . A lot of them think they are fit because of the image and they have a couple of tattoos on their arms and that.

(Unemployed roustabout, 39)

Combined with the availability of food 24 hours a day, this sort of behaviour can lead to the following consequences for some of the men. Commenting on taking charge of a team of electricians when he moved to a new company, an informant said:

I mean, I work with, sort of, five lads on a regular basis and when I first changed to this company . . . I thought they were all older than me

and, I found out, you know one I'd got to know them . . . I'm the
oldest. You know, I'm talking about lads – fat, bald . . . you know, I
was shocked.

(Electrician, 34)

Whilst another recalled that:

We have two working with us [apprentices] who weigh 17 stone each
and they both smoke and they are both 22 or 23 and they look old for
their time.

(Derrick hand, 35)

Both types of distorted body image, the female parody and the prematurely
aged image were deemed to result from a 'lack of control' or a 'lack of care'
by these individuals.

Shame how some people just let themselves go and don't look after
themselves. It's a waste. Everyone knows someone who doesn't bother
how they lead their life.

(Teacher, 39)

A theme running throughout these accounts is that of weight, and, in
particular, being overweight. Being overweight is clearly manifested in body
image and, for the men in this study, does have some significance in terms
of spoiling male identity, in that it blurs the 'muscular' male outline. At
a more acceptable level for some participants it appears as 'middle-aged
spread', despite the fact that most would argue that they have not yet
reached middle age. Although there may be cultural and class variations,
for example in attitudes to the 'paunch', most informants in this study did
acknowledge that it was, or was likely to become, a feature that they would
rather not have. Yet management of weight through active dieting (something that men are not often recommended to do) is perceived as inappropriate, 'not manly', something a man should not be seen or acknowledge
doing. For example, some informants said that their wives had urged them
to attend Weight Watchers or Scottish Slimmers, but that there was no way
that they would go. Reasons given included that 'they're just for women'
and that 'if I went I'd be embarrassed'. It was not dieting *per se* that they
objected to. It was rather that the organization of group dieting schemes,
media coverage of dieting and health and advertising for dietary regimes
were so closely associated with women, with controlling the female body
form, and that for informants who were overweight to diet openly might
mark a tacit acceptance of having 'lost it', the received male body, and hence
of having compromised male identity. Further, any obsession with weight
in male friends and relatives which involved overt dieting – rather than
exercise and dieting – gave cause for concern, an extreme form of behaviour
analogous to the bodybuilder. One informant, talking of his father, said:

He seems to be obsessed with his weight, ken. Just now . . . he seems to be aufae' thin, ken. Well I think for a man to diet like that . . .

(Warehouse dispatcher, 31)

The interview transcripts were then reread to discover whether informants judged their own health in terms of the classification of body shapes and behaviours described above. Two sets of mediating explanations for not desiring the 'body beautiful' or feeling that they were not 'a real mess' emerge. The first of these explanations relates to the social roles and obligations, which they as men experienced and, more or less, embrace and which are located within a 'normal everyday body'. The second set of explanations is clustered within or around the experiential nature of their individual physical bodies. Crucially, these two sets of explanations appear to give empirical weight to that theoretical and historical literature which posits the existence of multiple readings of the body, both within and in the space around the corporeal individual body. Both of these conceptualizations are explored, in turn, in Chapter 4.

Summary

The men in this study shared similar ideas concerning the ways in which health was conceptualized. Health was seen as a resource or a reserve which is genetically inherited; physical and, to a lesser extent, mental fitness, through which the reserve of health can be improved or maintained; a sense of emotional, mental and/or physical well-being; physical appearance; and, absence of disease or illness. Health as health-related behaviours permeated all of these concepts. Health as behaviour(s) is the concept that health promoters usually work with. These concepts are also socially constructed inasmuch as they represent shared meanings for the men in this study. Such concepts have been well documented by others (d'Houtaud and Field 1984; Hunt and Macleod 1987; Blaxter 1990; Williams 1990; Mullen 1993; Saltonstall 1993; Backett *et al.* 1994; MacInnes and Milburn 1994). The point is that their appearance in a variety of studies over time underlines the degree to which they endure in lay discourse. Of more significance was the realization that the body could provide a key frame of reference for male experience of health.

It is within the broader context of contemporaneous public health policy concerns and the evolution of professional practice that this chapter set out to describe lay theorizing about health that was found in informant accounts. Analysis of those accounts revealed descriptions and evaluation of cultural notions of the body and health, particularly as mediated through a range of established 'health-promoting' behaviours. Specifically, informants used symbolic representations of the male body to evaluate others' health. However, they made distinctions between how they evaluated other bodies and how they evaluated their own body. Other bodies were evaluated in terms familiar to proponents of a 'healthy lifestyle' – in terms of behaviours that promoted health and those that did not. Their own body was judged in terms of the ability to fulfil everyday gendered roles such as worker, father, husband and mate; though having a 'normal everyday body'. How embodied experience contributes to the construction and maintenance of masculine identities in everyday life is an issue addressed in Chapter 4.

Note

1 Brief biographical details of these men are given at the end of this book.

THE MALE
BODY IN
EVERYDAY LIFE

In medical discourse, it could be argued that women experience physiologically grounded, though culturally mediated, significant events across the lifecourse – menstruation, pregnancy, menopause (see discussion of the embodied and gendered lifecourse in the Introduction) – which could provide a bridging point for a transfer between production of health for the self and production of health for the body. The male informants in this study appear to lack such bridging points. In a health-promotion context such bridging points provide 'windows' for offering advice, information, skills and support to promote healthy lifestyles. However, for the men in this study social and cultural lifecourse transition events and status, such as marriage and parenthood, appear to mark points of closure and the start of a process of 'letting go' or 'losing' the physical body. This appears to be paralleled by the development of a social body and increased contexts and spaces in which the latter can be expressed. Underpinning this process is the gradual constraining of the physical body by economic and social obligations. As will be described, these obligations would appear to legitimize the 'blurring' of the idealized male form, particularly in its youthful incarnation so prevalent in the images used to promote consumer goods and services to men. An implication may be that it is OK to 'become' middle-aged and, for example, to acquire 'middle-aged spread', as long as an individual is able to experience his 'social' body through its presence, functioning or otherwise, in the social world.

Masculinity and social practice

The impact of marriage

When talking of their own or experiences of friends, participants would often mark marriage as a time of 'settling down' or 'letting go'. The consequences of this for health and the body are significant since for some informants there is a perception that marriage is equated with loss of control or 'losing it'.

> Once they get married I would say the majority of men seem to [be] happy with what they've got, ken? They seem to settle down and just let themselves go, ken. That's probably how you get a lot of men that are overweight, misshapen and what have you, ken, it's 'cause they let themselves go . . . Now when I was single, ken . . . fitter, when I was doing a lot more exercises. Once the football training stopped and I stopped playing my golf . . . if you get married you don't, you dinna really have the same time for doing these things, ken? Especially when you've got two young kids, and I think that's where I . . . the majority of people lose it. They don't have the same time for doing what they used to do.
>
> (Warehouse dispatcher, 31)

This informant is making an important point about 'facticity' of the body. He is able to observe it in others. At the same time, he advances the idea that to settle down socially can be linked to a physical 'settling down'. As will be discussed in the next chapter, this 'settling down' may be marked by a change in the nature of one's embodiment. The 'normal everyday body' may increasingly be perceived as a functional (indeterminate shape) body rather than as a physical (defined shape) body. It may therefore be relatively easy for informants to explain how they are able to accommodate themselves to the 'letting go' of the physical body; similarly, having children may be an ideal justification for women not to care any longer. In this sense informants may be relaying something about the cultural appropriateness of particular behaviours and presentation of the self.

For some informants this accommodation marks a transition in status as marriage marks the end of their 'wild youth', a period of masculinity-affirming behaviour – real or imagined:

> it's almost recognizing that your wild youth is over – putting it to sleep and giving it a decent burial. Maybe I was grieving over it in my early thirties – I've got it out of the way. Just getting old, who cares?
>
> (Teacher, 39)

By contrast, another informant, who had just separated from his wife, saw opportunities re-emerging:

you come home you get into a routine – there's nothing happening to my body. A few years ago I wasn't like this. Now I've got kids. I've got responsibilities and no gallivanting but, now I'm looking to get out and about . . . This time next year I will be a lot fitter . . . there will be nobody to tell me I'm playing too much golf.

(Builder, 33)

What is interesting about the above quote is the explicit reference he makes to his body – 'there's nothing happening to my body'. In referring to his physical body in this manner he perhaps reflects the observation that 'many men . . . sense the absence of the testing of strength that direct physical competition represents. They miss it as a ready affirmer of masculinity' (Gagnon 1974).

The role of fatherhood

Major factors in this loss of control are the perceived restrictions on time that marriage and fatherhood entail:

It restricted me from doing a lot of the things I used to do, especially when we started a family . . . It didn't change the way I felt about or what I wanted to do. It just restricted what I could do.

(Safety engineer, 31)

However, not all informants view fatherhood as a restriction. Looking back at their own childhood, some recall seeing very little of their own father because of work shift patterns or longer working days. A reaction to this is to want to spend more time with their children. Evenings and weekends become time for their relationship with the children. As the children grow, some fathers talk of the whole family going swimming or cycling. Very few respondents classed this as activity that would enable them to become fitter. Backett (1992b), in her study of middle-class families in Edinburgh, found that respondents would initially claim such family activity as exercise time for themselves whilst later acknowledging that such time was really just spent supervising children's activity.

Whilst the above accounts may be 'public' justifications – shared language categories – for not maintaining or adopting a certain health behaviour, one should be careful about denying their legitimacy. It is because these language categories are shared that they are legitimate. In the context of marriage and fatherhood it appears all too easy to 'lose' the opportunity to undertake exercise, a health practice which grounds male experience of health even fleetingly, in the body. Some informants who had given up taking part in sports after the birth of their children even described this in terms of 'making sacrifices', of 'having to sacrifice what I did before'.

The influence of work

This restricting or marginalizing of the physical male body appears to be woven into the fabric of everyday life, not just in a family context but also when informants are out at work. In the earlier chapter which explored informant concepts of health, informants who were in manual jobs would argue that fitness was obtained and maintained through their work and that such work exploited and relied on the maintenance of personal physical capital. However, those informants who were in non-manual occupations generally acknowledged that their work often acted to severely restrict opportunities or willingness to exercise. An informant who was previously quoted as being very conscious about his 'overweight' appearance and who finds that he does not have the energy to keep going at nights said:

> I am in at work at 7.30 a.m. and usually get away at 6.30 p.m. and have an hour off for lunch and nothing in between. It is more mental than anything else . . . I am coming home at nights now and I am tired . . . if I was a bit fitter I would be able to cope better with it and if I could cope with being less tired in the evening then I would be a bit more active in the evening.
>
> (Garage service manager, 32)

This leads to the idea that this informant only has open to him the possibility of experiencing his physical self and attendant opportunities for health practice at the margins and interstices of everyday working life. At its most extreme this may lead to acute distortion of the physical body in order to conform to the temporal structuring of the work environment. Another way of viewing this could be to argue that in order to achieve economic and social benefits an individual may choose to marginalize the physical body. This might be a strategy for neutralizing guilt that an informant might feel about not being able or willing to exemplify his masculine identity through the disciplining of his physical body. One informant, talking about his line manager, describes this phenomenon of marginalization in graphic terms:

> this man is five years younger than me. Weighs 20 stone. Doesn't have lunch. He comes in at 5.00 a.m. He works like a Trojan, he doesn't stop at lunchtime. If he does he goes round to Mr G——'s, no sandwiches or food. He lives on Coke ® during the day. Cans of Coke ® through the day to keep him going. He usually leaves work at 6.00 p.m. and goes straight into Mr G——'s and a few more pints. I don't think I have ever seen him eat. Not even a sweetie. I have seen him drinking cans of Coke ® all day . . . he smokes about 50 or 60 Marlborough during the time we are in work . . . He is so fat. He is just very large. He is always coughing and is 32. When I was told he was 32 I just could not believe it. I thought he was about 48 . . . I feel sorry for

the man because he is going to kill himself. He has got every single symptom of the heart attack . . . I mean I am a smoker and I think he cannot smoke more than that. He is at the limit. The human body cannot take any more.

(Technical design manager, 37)

Viewed from the perspective of cultural ideas about healthy and unhealthy bodies described previously (in Chapter 2), this individual has failed to balance his physical and social states. He presents a physical body which is a distortion of acceptable body forms. Even in his occasional lunch break or after work, the physical body is subsumed within the social context of drinking. One might agree with Martin's (1989) belief that men work (and socialize) in an 'abstracted conceptual mode', that the physical body becomes almost an irrelevance in the temporal and spatial structuring of public and private life, that its essence is distilled into a moral boundary between visceral processes and social order.

Of course, some of the men who participated in this study do actively experience their physical bodies through work and leisure. In general, the latter continue to do so because of a predisposition to engage the body actively in physical activity. This predisposition to physical activity was instilled as part of a regime of physical and moral development when at public school, in the armed forces or through active encouragement and enforcement by parents.

Accounts from those informants who work offshore, in the North Sea oil industry, suggest that it is the social construction of connections between family and work contexts that serves to marginalize the physical body and opportunities to engage physical modalities. This is exemplified by the comment of one informant who – in an echo of the Protestant work ethic – said of his father:

I've seen him work hard all his days. All my family worked hard all their days. To me you only get what you put in.

(Safety engineer, 31)

One informant, currently unemployed, a smoker, who previously had been a roustabout on the rigs, observed that:

Quite a few people use them [gymnasiums] but you tend to find that they are the guys who have not been using their bodies during the day – roustabouts, roughnecks and derrick men, they are not going to go down to the gym in the evening. They are knackered from working during the day. Instrument engineers, technicians, these sort of guys who have been sitting around on their bums all day, totally bored, they are the ones who use the gym. Again I think they have probably got a different sense of lifestyle . . . whereas . . . roughnecks and derrick men still tend to be the type of guys who are going to the pub, read the *Sun* and . . . betting. They still have the image they are working-class guys.

(Unemployed roustabout, 39)

Other offshore workers have commented that the offshore life, with its cycles of two weeks on and two weeks off, is an extreme social environment, in that those with families are completely separated from them. They have no social obligations that they are able to fulfil, whether as father or husband. As a social environment, the rigs are in a very real sense at a frontier between the social and natural worlds. The balance between the two is maintained through rigorous safety and working practices. In this environment, the worker's obligation is only to his job for the 12-hour shift during which he is on duty. The informant who works as an industrial chemist on the rigs and who regularly exercises in the gym also marks a distinction between use of the gym by manual and non-manual workers. Physical capital is acquired and expended by the former through the nature of their work. That same capital is acquired and expended primarily through exercise in the gym when off-shift by the non-manual workers. Even here, though, informants gave accounts of apprentices coming offshore for the first time, away from family, who when faced with the availability of four-course meals 24 hours a day would within months dramatically increase in weight.

For informants, the gradual elimination of physical body form as a defining feature of the social persona is most apparent as one moves into marriage and becomes a father. The assertion that marriage causes 'the majority of men' to 'lose it' does seem, in part, to refer to the physical expression of masculinity. This finds an echo in Brandes's (1980) ethnography of male sex and status in Andalusia. The notion that marriage, fatherhood and work may, in combination or separately, operate to constrain or distort the physical body whilst providing alternative contexts for constructing and projecting the social body (or persona) is found in participant accounts. The picture of marriage as a time of 'letting go' corresponds to Levinson's (1978) identification of the years between 33 and 40 as being a period of settling down. In an earlier section on 'health as a resource' it was argued that in the 'public' world of work individuals are morally obligated to maintain health in order to work. By contrast, Martin (1989) has shown that the private world of the home, where women predominate, operates according to more 'naturalistic' imperatives – tasks are not 'manufactured' or related primarily to the factory clock. So, when the men in this study (re-)enter the private domain of the home, fatherhood and marriage, they 'step out' of the public world. This crossing of boundaries into the private domain creates a situation in which the clarity of a public health morality, and a concomitant individual responsibility to maintain health, become fragmented by the necessity to 'fit in' with and satisfy a number of domestic imperatives such as family relationships, security, play and rest, and by the fact that certain health behaviours such as eating begin to assume primacy derived from the way they are locked into everyday life.

Physical bodies

All respondents felt or assumed the presence of their physical bodies. Previously, informants had spoken of health as appearance and social body types which were used to evaluate others' social health. What they were referring to was the embodied public personage in which the emphasis was on appearance – in terms of style and form – by which an individual is inserted into social contexts. By contrast, findings from this study suggest that in some respects the individual's physical body has an existence and a subjectivity of its own. This next section explores how informants perceive the individual-subjective-physical body and how it interacts with and stands apart from the public persona. Three dimensions of this relationship are introduced: body image as a template for the social persona; body maintenance; and damage and fragmentation.

Changing experience of the body

If informants hold images of their own bodies, their accounts tend to indicate that such images are representations of the physical body as it is remembered as being at points prior to assumption of the adult social self enmeshed in a web of social obligations. This memory of the body 'as it was' is found in participant narratives where they compare themselves now with how their body used to be 'as a kid', 'before I got married' or 'before I became a dad'. Whatever their current lifestyles and health-related behaviour, most informants did refer to a childhood in which the subjective physical (my) body was experienced and known through physical activity and sport. A car salesman, describing a working-class childhood, recalled:

> The physical side of things was great because . . . I was brought up in the generation where there wasn't the same amount of motor cars, so you could play in the streets and there was loads of kids where I was brought up. We were out playing all the time. Football, or just ball games. You were out playing all the time. Even when you came home from school. You used to go early in the morning so you could play football before you went in. You played football at lunchtime and then football at night before you came home. And once you had come home and had something to eat you went out in the evening – in the summer – and played again with the rest of the kids.
>
> (Car salesman, 36)

Informants who were raised in the crofting communities also recall long periods of physical activity – doing chores, going for walks, occasionally playing with other crofters' children. One informant, a white Trinidadian who smokes and works as a derrick hand on the rigs, sums up what this meant for the physical body. He said:

> I have a strong body. But that is because . . . when your body is forming and developing in your young days, and your body is starting to grow . . . it has all the necessary exercise it gets.
>
> (Derrick hand, 35)

For the few respondents who went to public school exercise was, as mentioned in the preceding chapter, acquired through being exposed to educational regimes which appear to have been based on the 'healthy mind in a healthy body' ethos. One informant recalled:

> I went to [Robert] Gordons . . . We had a swimming pool and three gyms . . . You were doing gym three times a week and swimming one afternoon each week. So it was an athletically-oriented education. If you wanted to do any sport you could get off any class you wanted – unless it was an exam – to go and do something to do with sport. A wee bit like the Navy. Same sort of idea. If you were good at sport in my school you could do no wrong. You got the yellow stripes around your blazer, and everything, you know.
>
> (Technical design manager, 37)

The subjective experiential body is one of the primary means by which most informants recall (or chose to recall) expressing themselves as social actors when young. It is the known body, the developing physical body through which these informants, as boys, recall experiencing their world. The natural body in Douglas's (1982) thesis is not yet a restricting medium of expression. Importantly, it is the site through which the developing social persona starts to emerge on to the social stage. As the individual passes through school, apprenticeship or college, relationships, work, marriage and parenthood, the image of the body-of-action is taken as the template, the image of his social identity, as he experiences it. It is what he draws upon to sustain his sense of self as he is drawn further on to the social stage. In turn, the natural body becomes the source of his resilience; it is tested and abused by the roistering excesses of a 'wild youth':

> played a lot of rugby, went to Majorca a lot. Played table tennis. Was a youth leader for a while. Yes, did a lot of healthy things but probably the booze and the fags counteracted it. You are young, so the body stands up to it, squeezing 25 hours into 24.
>
> (Teacher, 40)

In the process of abusing this physical body the individual acquires, develops and sustains the social self. In sum, memory of a younger 'naturally healthy' body interacts with masculine attitudinal and behavioural norms to 'construct' a template or 'personal fable' (Elkin 1984; Jack 1989) which sustains the individual's identity as a normal, socially healthy guy. It is in this sense that the apocryphal story is told:

> It is a mental thing. A man can live like a couch potato, he can drink 5 or 6 pints every 2 or 3 nights, he can eat all the unhealthy foods, but inside his head he . . . believes that he is . . . Rambo . . . he will try and do 20 or 30 press-ups and will probably damage himself.
>
> (Accountant, 40)

The gradual dislocation of body and self-image is not only grounded in a social and cultural context but finds expression in the ageing process:

> The things you did before with the greatest of ease are now not so easy . . . not as fast . . . age catching up. Apart from the obvious signs like losing hair, its not being able to judge the younger age quite too well. Depends what company I'm in what age I feel. I don't feel 37. Don't feel awful old. Depends who you're comparing the body with, how young it feels.
>
> (Quantity surveyor, 37)

Such accounts reveal how some of the participants experience or make sense of this disassociation of body and self-image. An often voiced attitude to this process of disassociation was one of fatalism, of inevitability:

> Stomach doesn't feel like it did 10 years ago. Getting inches here and there that won't go away. Can run and do weights but unless you're a kid, out there, running and twisting and turning, active all the time, it's no good.
>
> (Industrial chemist, 38)

In summary, informants develop as individuals, each in his own direction and at his own pace. As they make the transition from child to youth, youth to young adult and from there to mature adult, most gradually 'lose' everyday experience of the lived body actively experienced through physical activity. That they were once so active becomes part of the taken-for-granted nature of the body. The image that sustains such belief as the individual moves into work, marriage and fatherhood, appears to be the taken-for-granted body as they choose to remember it, particularly before becoming a father.

The role of body maintenance

When referring to the body, informants tended to use descriptions that used mechanical metaphors. For example, the heart was described as 'a pump'. Food (and occasionally drink) was described as 'fuel'. 'Energy' came from being fit, both mentally and physically. Mechanistic metaphors, as Martin (1989) notes, are employed by science and medicine to describe and dehumanize physiological and psychological processes, particularly as described by women. For example, giving birth is described as 'labour' and menstruation is 'failed reproduction'. The use of such metaphors in biomedical discourse serves to impose order on the body. Their appearance in lay narratives may be a reflection of their prevalence in the ways in which the popular mass media have taken this scientific discourse on board.

Whilst most informants used this style of discourse, they do not appear to accept the corollary that failure to adopt certain behaviours in order to develop a 'healthy' body is necessarily a matter of personal responsibility. When the issue of control and health behaviour was explored with informants, the primacy of health behaviours in body maintenance was challenged. Analysis of informant accounts reveals that the body itself was perceived to 'put itself in order', whilst health practices were used by the individual to 'manufacture' health or the appearance of health for self-image:

> I don't see any harm in occasional abuse of the body. I mean the human body can cope with it . . . if I've got a hangover I don't bother, just let the body get rid of the hangover.
>
> (Teacher, 39)

This notion appeared to be reinforced, for several of the informants, by explanations of treatment and cure that are recalled from conversations with their doctor. One informant, who had had some back trouble in the past year, asked his doctor why he had experienced a 'shooting pain' up his leg when standing up from putting away files in the bottom drawer of a filing cabinet at work. As he recalls the conversation:

> That happened. I mentioned that to him and he said well that was a good sign that if I was getting this reaction . . . then that . . . the nerves . . . were beginning to repair theirselves and that the nerves started from bottom and worked back this way.
>
> (Drilling equipment salesman, 38)

The notion of the body as maintaining itself also extends to the idea of a 'wise body', that the body will warn you if you attempt to exceed your or its capabilities:

> I'd like to do more than me body'll let me do, definitely yeah, mainly physical things which I would like to do. Probably things I've done in the past which I couldn't do now.
>
> (Teacher, 40)

> I always thought it was just my body saying, 'hey, just canny up a minute'.
>
> (Drilling equipment salesman, 38)

The ability of the body to maintain itself can be compromised through inappropriate and unrealistic body practices. One respondent, an amateur car mechanic, said:

> you know one of my hobbies is cars and working with engines, and every time you do something to make an improvement, it has an equal and an opposite effect. It messes something else up so that when you replace an engine with a, with a more highly powerful engine, instead of the engine breaking down, you start breaking down the gearbox. And then you put in a stronger gearbox, you then start breaking the transmission and the back axle. So I get the theory . . . that I sometimes think it's possible that the body is the same way.
>
> (Training consultant, 40)

Put more pithily by another respondent, 'If it works don't fix it!'. This perspective, in part, allowed the participant quoted above to rationalize why, although a smoker, he did not need to stop smoking. More generally, this notion, held by several of those participants who were either smokers, who did no exercise, or who ate 'unhealthy' foods with relish, may operate to sustain 'unhealthy' behaviours. In the same way the ageing process or the genetically programmed life-span of body elements is eventually perceived to affect the body's ability to maintain itself. The same informant went on to say that:

> There comes a stage in everybody when the body is going to stop fixing itself. Em . . . because the bit that did the fixing breaks down . . . or the healing at 50–60 might take longer or not be as effective as with a 10-year-old.
>
> (Training consultant, 40)

By contrast, some participants who consciously followed dietary or exercise regimes felt that

> healthy lifestyles help the body function properly. If you're overweight it puts a strain on your system and so makes it more likely to go wrong.
>
> (Mechanical engineer, 37)

In some instances, informants who exercised on an occasional and a regular basis acknowledged that even the fitness achieved through physical activity was, at their – relatively early – age starting to be tempered by the ticking of a 'biological clock'. One informant, who plays squash twice a week, made a qualitative distinction between why the body takes time to recover after strenuous physical exertion when a teenager aged 17 and seventeen years later:

Interviewee (I): I like to be able to do what I do. I play squash and don't like to feel at the end of the game like I am really just dead.

Researcher (R): When you say feel dead, what does that feel like?

I: Feeling so tired you are practically physically sick from exhaustion. Not ill-exhausted but physically exhausted. When I used to swim I was practically there several times and it is not a nice feeling. That was when you were pushed all the time. You were young and your body recovers. Now it takes a good while to recover. Now if I have a hard game of squash it takes a bit longer to recover and that is the bit I don't like. It comes with age.

(Software engineer, 34)

Ultimately though, among most participants this realization does not necessarily lead to the adoption of healthier body practices. Again, employing the principle 'if it works don't fix it', the body was described as:

Something I never bother with. It just ticks away nicely until it breaks down.

(Technician, 32)

An implication of this finding is that a man – advised at the screening clinic to reduce intake of fat and take some exercise as a way of losing some weight – may assess the relevance of such advice in terms of a social self-image (positive) rather than the actual condition of his body (negative), and so be weakly motivated to consider changing behaviours. This may be particularly the case where the body has become marginalized by the demands of work and family, and where there is a belief that if the body appears to be working then you should not tinker with it.

Damage and fragmentation

The way in which informants referred to the physical body in the section above demonstrates an almost implicit faith that at some very basic level the body acts to heal, perpetuate and reproduce itself. This working of the body on itself persists, even in the face of the marginalization of the physical body in an informant's social environment. At the same time the efficiency of the body in its concern with itself is gradually impaired by age, injury and the effects of illness or disease that together 'wear down' the body.

Many informants recount instances when the physical body, or more often a part of it, is damaged. The legacy of such damage becomes the notion that the fabric of the body is fragmented such that whilst at one level, they remain healthy or 'fit' in a social sense – and this is balanced by the endurance of key physiological and psychological processes and systems – yet in-between, their physical sense of maleness is chipped away at. In consequence, they may claim that 'I am fit but because of that accident that broke my leg the legs will never be really fit again'. Here is the idea that parts of the body become weakened whilst other parts remain strong.

The following accounts reveal something of the hidden burden of injury carried by informants in day-to-day life – hidden in the sense of not being revealed to a doctor or other health professional until perhaps much later on. The injuries recounted by informants are mainly musculoskeletal in nature. For example, at the start of the third and final interview with the following informant, I was asking how he had been keeping since we had last talked, and, in particular, how he was getting on with building an extension to his house, a project that had started just before the second interview and which he was carrying out with the help of his father and father-in-law. At the time of the second interview he had just 'strained' an elbow.

> *Interviewee (I)*: Feel quite comfortable and don't get many illnesses . . .
>   need to be nearer 60 before you start worrying about these things.
>   More likely to pull a muscle – minor aches and pains.
> *Researcher (R)*: How's the elbow these days?
> *I*: Didn't get any treatment for it at first. Got this gel, maybe stopped
>   using it before I fully recovered. Maybe just a weakness.
> *R*: Why did you not get treatment at first?
> *I*: It was a bit sore and it gave me a bit of bother now and then, but it
>   wasn't hugely significant.
> *R*: You said maybe it's just a weakness?
> *I*: Something I damaged that may not be as strong as it was in the first
>   place . . . probably the physical work, I was subjecting it to a good
>   deal more stress than the other parts.
>
>   (Warehouse manager, 35)

In this account the informant believes that the injury to his elbow may have occurred because it is 'weaker' than other parts of his body that were exposed to the same strain by digging out the foundations. The explanation for this weakness is that the elbow is 'something I damaged' previously and so was not as strong as the rest of his body. At the same time, this explanation for the strain was sufficient not to require him to go to the doctor for an alternative explanation, particularly since it did not incapacitate him in any major way. When he did eventually get treatment, he bought an over-the-counter product from a local pharmacy.

The informant below has a similar kind of 'strain', this time to his shoulder.

> *Interviewee (I)*: I've damaged my shoulder. I think that was since I saw
>   you last . . . pulled some muscles or tendons in my shoulder and it's
>   still not healed yet.
> *Researcher (R)*: How did you do that?

I: I did it playing cricket for the first time in something like 10 years. I bowled three overs and my shoulder wasn't used to the strain . . . It's a niggling sort of thing. Stopping me doing a lot of things that I would want to do.

R: Right. Such as?

I: Well, racquet sports: tennis, badminton. And I also have to think, any activity that I do, I have to think whether it's going to hurt my shoulder or set it back.

(Solicitor, 39)

In this instance, the explanation for the cause of the injury is that it happened because of a lack of practice: the 'shoulder wasn't used to the strain'. What is interesting about this explanation is that the informant plays a lot of racquet sports which involve use of the shoulder muscles. Yet he does not look for an explanation in the strain that he exposes his shoulder muscles to through regular exercise. The injury occurred because he subjected his shoulder to the rigours of bowling three overs in a cricket match. The injury did not stop him working, though it did put a stop to other sports that use the shoulder muscles. It also makes him think before doing any other activity such as lifting, which may prolong the strain. In this instance, the weakness of the shoulder is not seen to result from previous injury but from a lack of practice in undertaking a particular manoeuvre. Again, he did not consult his doctor.

In this next example, I was asking the informant at his second interview how his football training was going.

Interviewee (I): I have missed quite a bit. Haven't played for three weeks. It is a thigh muscular injury. Went to the physio for the last three weeks. Canna seem to get it better.

Researcher (R): What happened?

I: No idea. It was before my holidays. I felt this strain in the front of my thigh – didn't think much about it and played away – it got sore and the next week I played again and it got worse. I thought during my holidays it would get rest but I came back, played a game and it was the worst ever so got treatment and haven't played since . . . For once I'm doing what I'm told – I'm just a bit wary. I feel that if I went back against her advice and something happened . . . I'd rather wait till she said give it a go . . . it's just nae right.

(Electrician, 33)

This informant had previously acknowledged that the injuries sustained by and the stresses to which he subjected his body through playing football might weaken certain parts such as the knees and the ankles, making them more vulnerable to arthritis at some point in the future. In the instance quoted above he adopted two opposite strategies in getting rid of the injury.

In the first, he decided to actively 'work' the injured area by playing another game of football. When this did not work, he used a family holiday to rest the injury. His action in playing football again as soon as he returned from holiday may have been motivated by the idea that the injury had 'gone away'. But it had not, and his experience of it was qualitatively worse than on previous occasions. At this point he realizes that he cannot rely on the body to 'put itself in order' so he seeks treatment from a physiotherapist and follows her advice in how to deal with the injury. Again, his concern throughout this episode is not with the impact that the injury might have on work or the family, but that it might stop him playing football – which, temporarily, it does in the end.

The previous three accounts illustrate the notion of a localized and specific weakness of a part of the body. In the following account the informant, recovering from an operation to remove a brain tumour, talks about a more generalized weakening of those aspects of body function controlled by the brain, such as vision, or close to the site of the tumour, such as deafness in his left ear.

> *Interviewee (I)*: I was only aware that it was there for a few weeks. Before it was removed I was told it was a growth behind my left ear. Other people made that connection. I thought it was just a lump inside here which had to be removed. Other people knew it was a growth inside the brain. If I had thought about that I would have been worried about it. The thought of going in for the operation was cause for concern and how you would leave the operating theatre – that worried me – the fact that I may wake up during the operation totally aware of what is going on and not be able to communicate with anybody. The thought of dying never entered my head . . . I didn't realize it would take as long to recover from the operation as it did . . . With hindsight I can see why they [the doctors] didn't because it takes so long and if they did tell you it could take 2 or 3 years that could have a very demoralizing effect.
>
> *Researcher (R)*: What do you mean by the recovery taking 2 or 3 years?
>
> *I*: Not being able to see properly, not being able to talk properly or swallow properly or walk in a straight line – or control your walking. All those things gradually went away to a certain extent. . . . I'm as recovered as I'm ever going to be. Balance is never going to be what it was. I will always have double vision and [be] deaf in my left ear. My hair will never be any better than it is now. I think I've reached a plateau – from here it doesn't get any better.
>
> (Engineer, 38)

This informant manifests surprise when talking about the duration and nature of the recovery. He achieved a gradual recovery of functions – talking, swallowing, walking – up to a point. He then expresses a sense of fatalism that 'from here it doesn't get any better'. The body he has now is not the body that he had before his operation. In its abilities and capacities, the physical body is less than it was. Even so, he was able to return to work, though now with an altered perception of his body.

In the next account, the informant's explanation for his recurring sinus problem is that it is exacerbated by 'critical work problems'.

> Sinus infection is unlikely to kill me. Might feel bloody awful, but when I've had a bad nose infection this year it really was because of critical work problems. Couldn't just go to bed and say I wasn't coming in . . . You feel a wally coughing, spluttering and sneezing. It isn't life threatening.
>
> (Accountant, 40)

Here the physical problem is chronic, but the informant continues to work because: the problem is 'unlikely to kill me'; there were 'critical work problems' that the informant felt he had to be able to resolve; and the symptoms – 'coughing, spluttering and sneezing' – were not sufficient to legitimatize taking time off. Of the three explanations offered, the first and third could be said to relate to a masculine imperative to play down the impact of illness when discussing it with another man. In some respects, though, it appears that the second explanation is the key one. If a man, socially, is defined more by his work nowadays than, for example, by physical strength or courage in battle, then to have his capacity to affirm his identity through work circumscribed or curtailed by illness or injury exposes him to the danger of losing that identity. Another informant put this predicament clearly when he said: 'If you can't cope that's when you start to fall apart.' Eales (1989), in an exploratory study of unemployed men, concluded that although shame was common among unemployed men in his study it was not universal. He hypothesized that its occurrence might be explained by emotional sensitivity to stigma.

One informant, a diabetic, gives an account that reveals something of the interplay between his permanently constrained physical body and his social environment.

> If only I could get rid of this diabetes. To me it is the biggest ball and chain I have ever had to endure . . . if I wasn't diabetic my whole life would be completely different. Goodness knows where I'd be now – I would be lying in the sand in the Gulf as a skeleton by now. If I wasn't a diabetic I would feel good when I woke up in the morning, which I don't. This morning I woke up and I felt so rough. S—— said to me: 'Go and phone the doctor or something'. But I haven't mentioned this to the doctor or the consultant, that I feel so bad in the morning. I just cannot straighten up and open my eyes. I feel ill. I felt sick this morning . . . I mentioned it to a diabetic at work in passing. We tend

not to talk to each other about it at work. I don't know why, I am quite willing to talk about it. I said to this guy in my last job, 'Do you feel rough in the mornings?' and he said 'Do I ever!' . . . I would really like to get rid of it. It rules your whole life. It ruled what I ate for tea tonight. It is quite incredible how it rules your life.

(Technical design manager, 37)

The condition of diabetes has removed the taken-for-granted nature of a physical body that maintains itself. In trying to control the diabetes he treads a very fine line between having to look after his own physical body and having his physical condition threaten his ability to affirm himself, his sense of identity. This is perhaps best summed up by another informant, who said:

You can work all your life and you become ill and you can no longer pay for everything and you lose everything rapidly.

(Industrial chemist, 38)

The body and health

This chapter has, so far, explored the various ways in which informants share conceptualizations of the body in relation to health and in the context of everyday life. This final part of the chapter summarizes how informants conceptualize the body in relation to health. It also examines some of the ways in which these cultural ideas about the body verify and challenge existing treatment of the body in the mainly sociological and psychological literature on the body and self reviewed in Chapter 2.

In talking of the two bodies (the social and the physical) Douglas (1982) has argued that in the ongoing exchange of meanings the physical body is a very restricted medium of expression. Informant accounts appear to support this idea initially. The healthy other and the unhealthy other are described using three descriptive categories: shape (height, weight, fat distribution, muscle tone); stigmas (pallor, sweat, burst blood vessels); and lifestyle (alcohol consumption, eating, exercise, smoking, sleep, stress). The main differences between healthy and unhealthy bodies are that in the former the boundaries of the physical body appear to be obscured by an attempt to demonstrate a basic consonance between health behaviours and daily routine. As part of this, stigmas are absent and shape only generally defined. By contrast, in the latter, expansion or distortions of the physical boundaries begin to restrict the medium of expression of the 'social approved body'. Behaviours are referenced in order to explicate shape and stigmas. The physicality of the unhealthy body is paramount.

By contrast, in much of the theorizing about bodies there is an assumption that the physical/natural body exists primarily as a site for the investment of social order over individuals. Informant conceptualizations of the body – whilst supporting the idea of the existence of social and physical forms of embodiment and that the social body appears to operate as a wider medium of expression – also point to two differences with much social theorizing about the body. First, informants are thoroughly conversant with a public health discourse that aims to 'construct healthy bodies' but appear to put more emphasis on responsibility concerning the gendered nature of social roles and obligations. Second, their conceptualizations of the physical body (the memory of the body 'as it was', a body that 'fixes itself', and the fragmentary nature of their experience of the physical body through illness and disease) are far more prominent both in themselves and the impact that they have on informants' responses to the discourse on healthy bodies and healthy lifestyles than is suggested by the literature.

The emergent nature of the physical body and the emphasis on personal responsibility in relation to social practice as distinct from personal responsibility for health point towards a dialectical nature of embodiment such as that espoused by Elias (1978), Giddens (1991) and Shilling (1991). In informant accounts, the nature of that intercourse appears to be pragmatic, ambiguous and highly contingent. In particular, it will be suggested in the following chapter that the facticity of individual embodiment may operate to neutralize the public health discourse on risk and the promotion of healthy bodies.

The key to seeing the relationship between physical and social bodies as problematic is found in the way informants conceptualize their own physical body. That is, the individual does not objectify his own body. At a physical level, his body has an existence and subjectiveness of its own. This is different, for example, from Saltonstall's (1993) findings from an American sample, which she felt demonstrated that men had a 'power-over' relationship to their bodies, that their bodies 'belonged' to them the same as an object belongs. This notion of a 'power-over' relationship between a man and his body comes across as more tenuous when informant accounts are considered. An explanation could be that the men in this study exercise control over and through the social self – which, as perceived by some informants, is itself based on a subjective image of the physical body – rather than through the physical body itself.

Saltonstall (1993: 10–11) has also stated that the 'production of health for the self involves personal responsibility for "body maintenance"'. This is drawn from a notion prevalent since the sixteenth century that the body is like a machine (Beaune 1989) and so requires maintenance to control or mediate the effects of ageing, disease and abuse of the body. Similarly, this conceptualization was evident in the government advertisement promoting individual responsibility for health under its *Health of the Nation* initiative referred to in Chapter 3. Such maintenance, Saltonstall (1993: 10–11) argues, is the product of body practices defined by mechanistic metaphors to describe the inputs to and effects of healthy eating, exercise, moderate alcohol consumption, not smoking and getting enough rest, on the body. Yet, informants' perception of their own physical embodiment as having a largely independent existence from the social self also serves as a rationalization against accepting personal responsibility for one's own body. Informants would shrug and say that 'you've got what you've got' or 'you're just the weight you are'. In addition, the positing of a 'normal everyday body' in response to images of the ideal 'healthy' male would suggest that this constitutes almost a form of resistance to social pressure to adopt certain health-promoting behaviours. Thus, whilst the thinking behind the government campaign may have been both 'medically' and ideologically 'correct', it was culturally – for these informants – ill informed.

It is part of the ambiguous nature of the relationship between physical and social modes of embodiment that physical form continues to operate as a social marker of health. Yet on a personal basis it appears to have been supplanted among informants by the everyday imperative to socially gendered practice: work (employee or employer), fatherhood and husband. Informants problematize the physical–social relationship in other, more specific, ways. For example, responsibility for sustaining the social persona through work, sport and family is achieved at a cost to the physical body. At one level, the costs incurred appear minor and transitory – breaking a leg in a motorcycle accident or 'getting the flu', conditions which the social persona recovers from. At another level, the onset of diabetes or diagnosis of a brain tumour may have more fundamental effects on the ability of the individual to affirm his masculine identity through the social body.

Similarly, at one level, informants think of the physical body as an enduring, almost a taken-for-granted entity. At another level, the physical body is experienced in a sporadic fashion, apart from instances where chronic disease perpetuates awareness and action within the confines of the physical body. This notion of the physical body constraining the social body, of limiting what may have become the taken-for-granted routines and opportunities of everyday life, has been comprehensively examined (Murphy 1987; Kleinman 1988). There are instances, though, when informants appear actively to manage the relationship between their physical and social selves. Informants who took relatively little exercise spoke of how the pursuit of the 'body beautiful' can be achieved, but at a cost to the social self. It is in this context that the relationship between the social self and the physical body is explicitly stated by one of the informants who, from his accounts, sustains a regular and intensive exercise regime:

It is all about motivation. Because as soon as you start your body says 'wait a minute I have had enough of this, let's sit down and have a rest'. But if you push yourself past that then the next day you go a bit further and you start enjoying it . . .

(Industrial chemist, 38)

Finally, one should acknowledge that the social body itself may be a problematic mode of embodiment for some informants. Mullen (1993), in an extension of Crawford's thesis of the operation of modes of control and release through the social body, has demonstrated that the men in his study did employ strategies to find temporary release – in smoking and drinking – from the temporal ordering of the domestic and work environments. Although data in the current study have not been analysed with a view to uncovering accounts of similar strategies, the notion of desiring change, of seeking release at least from presenting the social body in the public work-space, was articulated by a few informants. At a very fundamental level, one informant said:

> I am under an awful lot of pressure in my job on a day-to-day basis which my wife doesn't fully appreciate, and I won't take it home to her because I don't think it's fair to burden her as well as me. That's the reason why I have to have a switch-off period at some point during the day. . . . I have worked for 20 years now, but I would love to take 6 months off and do something I wanted to do. Whether it be to build a workshop at the bottom of the garden in the shed and make furniture or whatever. Just to do something like that, where there is no mental pressure at all. You are in charge of yourself and could work at your own pace and do your own things.
>
> (Teacher, 40)

In sum, informants appear to present notions of the body and health in which symbolic and pragmatic elements exist as cultural categorizations 'which structure the world into a system of differences into which the body and self is placed' (Falk 1994). The existential ground of this flux between categories is the embodied individual. It is to the idea of embodiment and the development of a grounded theory analysis of the empirical data presented in the previous two chapters that the next chapter turns.

CHAPTER 5

THE IDEA OF
EMBODIMENT

In establishing a space for understanding how masculinities and health practices come together, I would suggest that embodiment provides the ground on which the dynamics of gender are made personal and the tensions of agency and structure are realized. As such, this chapter looks at the theoretical basis for treating embodied everyday experience as a critical theoretical and practical issue, one that public health and health promotion specialists – rightly advocating action to address the social and economic determinants of health – need to grapple with.

Exploring Mauss's (1989) distinction between the social person (*personne*) and the individual self (*moi*) provides a starting point for understanding that embodiment locates the relationship between structure and agency at an individual level – as it also does by resolving the problem of given dichotomies such as individual/society, male/female, public/private. In doing so, it is suggested that embodiment can be viewed as the everyday location of practice which facilitates 'the interweaving of personal life and social structure' (Connell 1987: 61) and which, specifically, has salience in the context of the investigation and placement of lay knowledge. To this end, the concept of embodiment discussed and delineated in this section draws, most particularly, upon the work of Thomas Csordas (1990, 1993, 1994).

Before turning to the concept itself, the salience of embodiment can be explained in terms of the relationship that pertains between the body/self and time. Merleau-Ponty (1962: 70) has said that the body is our point of insertion into the world, our point of view upon the world. In anthropology, time is a 'carrier of significance' (Fabian 1983: ix). In the context of every-day life, time is 'anthropocentric' like the space in which it takes place (Heller 1984: 239). In this sense, everyday life is said to relate to the 'here and now' of a person. For the purposes of everyday knowledge, time is con-nected with the practical business of orientation, that is, praxis or practice. Thus practice occurs at the point of our insertion into the world. At that point of insertion we do not perceive ourselves as other than we are. Young (1980: 140) comments that 'it is the ordinary purposive orientation of the body as a whole toward things and its environment which initially defines the relationship of a subject to its world'. This is not to propose that we constantly attend to, or are aware of, our bodies as material, physical and biological entities. What it does suggest is that, as researchers or health professionals, we need to be aware of their presence.

Embodiment, not bodies

Plessner (Honneth and Joas 1988), from the perspective of philosophical anthropology, makes the distinction between *der Leib* and *der Körper* as signifying twin modalities of the 'lived body'. *Der Leib* is unique to the German language, and refers to a particular 'living' experiential body, whereas *der Körper* describes the 'objective, exterior and institutionalised body' (Turner 1992: 41) more familiar to Western culture. Together, they enable one to perceive the ambiguous nature of embodiment, as encom-passing objective and subjective realities; nature and society; personal and impersonal experience; interior and exterior states. Turner (1992: 42) argues that the *Leib/Körper* distinction is a fundamental contrast to the Cartesian legacy in sociology (and, it could be argued, in contrast to the Cartesian legacy in Western science more generally), which has usually identified the human body as *der Körper* rather than as simultaneously *Leib* and *Körper*.

The *Leib/Körper* distinction is a central theoretical perspective which informs further discussion of embodiment in this chapter and, in particular, in a gendered form may be of critical relevance to the operationalization of the body within a theory of social practice, such as that enunciated by Bourdieu (1977) and Connell (1987). In using the *Leib/Körper* sense of the human body – what Plessner refers to as the 'organismal body' and the 'objectual-instrumental body' (Honneth and Joas 1988: 87) or what Turner describes as the 'body-for-itself' and the 'body-in-itself' (Turner 1992: 42) – however, there are problems. This distinction of the being of the body lacks a clear idea of how these twin modalities of the body interact with each other and with other bodies in creating and sustaining an individual's iden-tity in and experience of the world. In part, this may derive from Plessner's general orientation to his subject. Turner (1992: 43) suggests that Plessner is guided by a phenomenological concept of experience rather than empirical evidence. It is suggested that it is a person's gendered identity, which inter-penetrates both *der Leib* and *der Körper*, which becomes the precondition for human agency.

Elsewhere, Terence Turner (1980: 112) has coined the term 'the social skin' – the common frontier of society, the social self and the psychobiological individual to describe the point at which the social and physiological modes of embodiment meet. According to Turner it is the symbolic stage upon which the drama of socialization is enacted. However, Giddens (1991: 99) describes the body as 'an action system, a mode of praxis' with its 'practical immersion in the interactions of day-to-day life' being an 'essential part of the sustaining of a coherent sense of self-identity'. This latter perspective provides a focus, in public health, for a more empirical investigation of the relationship between embodiment, gender and health. In a similar vein, Lawler (1991: 5) has argued that when nurses deal with the bodies of other people 'they operate from a knowledge base which is interpretative, contextual, and integrative of subject and object'. She refers to this as a *somological* approach. In essence it is about embodiment. Csordas (1993: 138) has commented, in this respect, that 'somatic modes of attention are culturally elaborated ways of attending to and with one's body in surroundings that include the embodied presence of others'. The key point to make is that embodiment is not about the representation of bodies, nor is its focus simply the material, biological body; rather Csordas (1993: 135) has defined it as 'perceptual experience and the mode of presence and engagement in the world'.

This approach to the living body starts with the premise that the body is understood as the existential or personal ground of culture. As such, it is about being, not representation:

> As applied to anthropology, the model of text means that cultures can be understood, for purposes of internal and comparative analysis, to have properties similar to texts . . . In contrast, the paradigm of embodiment means not that cultures have the same structure as bodily experience, but that embodied experience is the starting point for analyzing human participation in a cultural world.
>
> (Csordas 1993: 135)

Csordas's paradigm of embodiment is defined through a critical examination of two existing theories of embodiment: the phenomenological approach of Merleau-Ponty, who articulates embodiment as the problem of perception; and Bourdieu, who locates embodiment in a discourse of practice. For Merleau-Ponty the main duality in the domain of perception is that of subject/object. For Bourdieu, the principal duality in the domain of practice is structure/practice. A common concern is not to mediate these dualities but to collapse them by invoking the methodological principle of embodiment (Csordas 1990: 8). Merleau-Ponty's position is perceived to be a critique of empiricism in that our starting point should be the experience of perceiving, because we do not have any objects prior to perception. Bourdieu's goal is to collapse the dualities of body/mind in the concept of habitus, the locus of which is 'the conjunction between the objective conditions of life, and the totality of aspirations and practices completely compatible with those conditions' (Csordas 1990: 11). Csordas (1990: 12) suggests that these two approaches represent the 'paradox of positions compatible within the paradigm of embodiment, but articulated in the methodologically incompatible discourses of phenomenology and . . . dialectical structuralism'. He goes on to suggest that within a paradigm of embodiment analysis should not focus on perceptual categories or questions of classification/differentiation but on the body-as-subject in experiential terms. Thus,

> [w]hen both poles of the duality [biology and culture] are recast in experiential terms, the dictum of psychological anthropology that all reality is psychological . . . no longer carries a mentalistic connotation, but defines culture as embodied from the outset
>
> (Csordas 1990: 37)

In many respects this position is reflected in the work of others, such as Jung (1976), Johnson (1987), Lakoff (1987) and Freund (1988). For example, Lakoff argues, from the perspective of experiential realism, that reason is embodied and imaginative. Thus experience includes 'the internal genetically acquired makeup of the organism and the nature of its interactions in both its physical and social environments' (Lakoff 1987: xv). Jung (1976: 381) offers a riposte to Foucault – after developing an explanation of human behaviour that presupposes the phenomenon of the lived body – when he argues that

> the world is inhabited by embodied subjects and [drawing on Merleau-Ponty] Being-in-the-world is constituted by the body as an active subject (i.e. embodiment). If a body is an active agent, it must be argued that the self as having a body must also be an active agent.

This raises the possibility of the physiological body working on the social self as well as society ordering the body. The notion of the physical body constraining the social body, of limiting what may have become the taken-for-granted routines and opportunities of everyday life, has been comprehensively examined both in medical sociology and in the literature on disability. Exploring the role of personal illness narratives in the context of doctor–patient interaction, Kleinman (1988: 45) commented: 'The fidelity of our bodies is so basic that we never think of it – it is the certain grounds of our daily experience'. Murphy reflected upon the shattering of Merleau-Ponty's mind–body system in the context of his own experience of a benign tumour on the spinal cord. When first told of the diagnosis, his reaction was one of amazement and awe (Murphy 1987: 2).

The principle of indeterminacy

Underlying Csordas's paradigm of embodiment is the notion that indeterminacy is an essential element of existence. He does not say that indeterminacy as a concept can, or should, necessarily be applied to the analytical process, but attempts to offer some theoretical grounds for 'accepting it as an inevitable background condition of our analyses' (Csordas 1993: 150). He attempts to trace some of its defining features with reference to Merleau-Ponty and Bourdieu. In the work of Merleau-Ponty he finds indeterminacy in the act of 'transcendence'. That is, 'Merleau-Ponty sees in the indeterminacy of perception a transcendence that does not outrun its embodied situation, but that always 'asserts more than it grasps' (Csordas 1993: 150).

Regarding Bourdieu, Csordas (1993: 150) asserts that 'the synthesis of practical domains in a unitary habitus is likewise based on indeterminacy', but that this version of indeterminacy does not result in transcendence. Instead, his 'logical indeterminacy' becomes the basis for the 'transposition of different schemes into different practical domains' (Csordas 1993: 150), that is, it becomes the basis for regulated 'improvisation'. For Csordas, this is exemplified in Bourdieu's ethnography of the Kabyle (Bourdieu 1979) by the ambiguous ways in which male/female oppositions are applied to the interior/exterior of the household, its internal spaces and cooking utensils. In this sense, Csordas is directing us to where the principles of indeterminacy may be operating rather than providing a determinate and finished concept.

Elsewhere, Merleau-Ponty's concept of the *chiasmatic relationship* – as discussed and elaborated by Leder (1990) – between the surface body and underlying visceral processes would appear to elaborate other features of indeterminacy. Leder's exposition of the chiasmatic relationship proceeds from what he identifies as a limitation in Merleau-Ponty's (1962) notion of the primacy of body and perception, as contained in *Phenomenology of Perception*: that perception and the lived body should not be understood as one and the same thesis in terms of our relation to the world. For,

> [b]eneath the surface body, perceiving and perceived, acting and acted upon, lies an anonymous visceral dimension . . . My sensorimotor being-in-the-world rests upon a set of vegetative functions hidden from myself no less than from others. Within me proceed circulatory, digestive and respiratory pathways which resist the apprehension and control of the conscious 'I' and yet . . . sustain the 'I' at every moment.
>
> (Leder 1990: 209)

Leder (1990: 209) argues that by referring only in passing to these visceral processes (prenatality, sleep) Merleau-Ponty fails to articulate the impersonal horizons that in all directions outrun the body as perceiver. From this, Leder moves to a discussion of Merleau-Ponty's last unfinished work, *The*

Visible and the Invisible (1968), in which the terminology of the lived body is replaced by the ontological notion of 'flesh'. 'Flesh' is 'a kind of circuit, a coiling over of the visible upon the invisible which traverses me but of which I am not the origin' (Leder 1990: 210). Thus Merleau-Ponty proposes 'flesh' as the 'chiasmatic structure' and since he considers the human body to be an *exemplar sensible* – that is, a structure in which is contained and exhibited the general structure of the world – he proceeds in his analysis of the 'flesh' by examining the lived body. A number of chiasmatic relationships are then explored: body/world, self/other, visible/invisible. Taking the example of self/other, Leder (1990: 211) comments: 'My perspective and that of the other intertwine in mutual validation, while never quite coinciding. The reality of the world is secured via its presence to other eyes, other hands, than my own'.

What is interesting about this notion is that it suggests that embodiment/textuality may themselves be indeterminate analytical paradigms that are manifested and related through a chiasmatic relationship. In this sense, embodiment should be seen as complementary to the concern with discourse/textuality. It is in the work of Desjarlais (1992) that empirical evidence of this relationship can be sought. Deriving from his fieldwork with the Yolmo Sherpa of Nepal, he contends that a culturally constituted aesthetics of everyday life underlies moments of health, illness and healing. In an account which focuses on an illness experienced by one of his informants, Mingma, he concludes:

> The way in which Mingma wields his body or engages with others in everyday life seems more a matter of artistic 'composition' than of belief, symbol, or deep logical 'structure'. Any study of these compositions must come to terms with their meanings, but it must also assess the way in which cultural sensibilities assert particular values to those meanings and how, in turn, the values register, as felt qualities, within the everyday uses of bodies. [Thus] . . . [w]e must also consider how bodily and social experiences are variously composed within a cultural setting, and the moral, aesthetic and political 'building blocks' of these compositions.
>
> (Desjarlais 1992: 1116)

'Being in shape': an embodied concept of gendered health practice

In seeking to 'discover' what makes a healthy person, the emphasis should not be on how the body is constructed as text but on how cultural/public discourse and the embodied – and gendered – self may momentarily be 'put together' in the context of everyday life. On that basis, this chapter now turns towards defining a core grounded concept for analysing men's health practices derived from the interview data represented by those accounts presented in Chapters 3 and 4 and from observations carried out during a parallel study of a local well man clinic. This concept is then used in the next chapter to facilitate a theoretical analysis and interpretation of the well man clinic in order to show how individual agency interacts with and resists public health discourse and the clinic as forms of surveillance.

What the data demonstrate is a particular relationship that obtains between action by the men in this study and their social environment. Central to a better understanding of this relationship is the analytical concept of 'being in shape'. This concept and its subsidiary categories (male body schema, managing ambiguity and evaluating social fit-ness) are discussed below.

The aim of this section is to organize these categories in such a way as to illuminate the relationships that operate between them. In this, the purpose of analysis was not to 'uncover' some cultural universals nor is its stance that of extreme cultural relativism. Rather, the object was to develop a synthesizing analysis in which, to quote Geertz (1973: 44), 'biological, psychological, sociological, and cultural factors can be treated as variables within unitary systems of analysis'.

The motivation for this enterprise, the moving beyond but not away from informant accounts, is to make explicit the interpretation which I, as the researcher, had made of the data offered to me by the participants. Mindful of what Geertz (1973: 30) has termed 'the hard surfaces of life . . . [and] the biological and physical necessities on which these surfaces rest', the development of this particular core analytical category drew upon the axiom promoted by Csordas, in which the body is experienced as 'the existential ground of culture' (Csordas 1990: 5, 39) – the subject of culture rather than an object in relation to culture.

Accordingly, 'being in shape' is defined as an analytical concept – situated within the theoretical paradigm of embodiment – which provides an interpretation of how the men in these studies experienced and made sense of personal health. That is, to adapt Connell (1987: 63), how, in a health context, masculinity is organized as a going concern. As a framework it shows that physical affirmation of masculinity is often impracticable in the context of everyday life. Indeed, the physical body has become so marginalized for many of the men I talked with that it flickers in and out of their lives, potentiated and unpredictable.

Figure 5.1 shows the principal relationships within the concept 'being in shape'. I have represented the concept schematically because it did not seem possible, or desirable, artificially to separate out categories which appear interdependent. It is not possible to speak of 'a male body'. Just as Segal (1990) and Connell (1995) have posited the existence of multiple masculinities, so is masculinity embodied in a number of ways within an individual and his social environment. A category 'male body schema' which has four

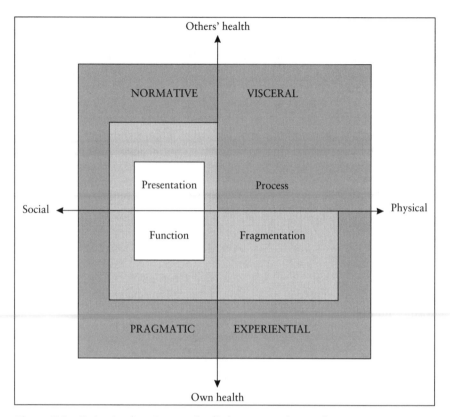

Figure 5.1 'Being in shape': an embodied concept of masculinity

main dimensions, or modes of embodiment, is therefore proposed, based on informant conceptualizations of embodiment reported in Chapters 3 and 4. These are: normative embodiment; pragmatic embodiment; experiential embodiment; and visceral embodiment.

In referring to schema, Feher's preference for 'modes of construction' rather than 'representation' is adopted. In distinguishing between the two he commented that:

> the history of its [the body's] representations . . . always refers to a real body considered to be 'without history' – whether it is the organism observed by natural sciences, the body proper as perceived as phenomenon, or the instinctual, repressed body on which psychoanalysis is based – whereas the history of its modes of construction can, since it avoids the . . . massive oppositions of science and ideology or of authenticity and alienation, turn the body into a thoroughly historicised and completely problematic issue.

> (Feher 1989: 11)

The distinction between representation and construction is stressed because, for the informants in this study, the embodied self and the bodies of others that they describe are historical and subjective forms. They are embedded within and to an extent are constructed by, explanatory narrative histories of the self and the other.

Normative embodiment

Although I have previously referred to body 'stereotypes' earlier in this chapter, upon reflection, the term *normative embodiment* is adopted. This is because the images of healthy and unhealthy others that were offered to the researcher were not simple lifeless representations. Although presentational, in the sense that 'first impressions matter', quite clearly the unhealthy other, and to a lesser extent, the healthy other, were presented as lived modes of construction. Each consisted of a more or less generalizable narrative that provided explanation for how a particular body shape may have been achieved and is maintained.

Such body shapes have currency as symbolic modes for explicating and transmitting cultural and social values regarding masculinity and health. In this study, the informants identified body shapes that they used to make judgements about the health or lack of health of other men. In psychological parlance, these shapes are variations on the ectomorph/mesomorph/endomorph continuum discussed in Chapter 1.

Informants' reactions to the body image in the advertisement shown in Figure 3.1 suggest that the mesomorphic standard was perceived as an inherently artificial creation: masculine certainly, but at the margins of what most informants perceive to be the everyday social contexts of embodied male identity. At the margins of male identity, the mesomorphic body also teeters on the edge of ill health, relying on asocial medicophysical regimes to develop and maintain the 'hard edges' of masculine definition. Aspiring to such a body may have cultural value in constraining and defining a male/female dichotomy. Paradoxically, it can also involve an opting out of the lived temporal and spatial social ordering of masculinity in order not just to obtain an ideal body shape but also to subvert contemporary gender practices.

Less surprisingly, the endomorphic body is generally also perceived as being both less masculine and unhealthy. Whilst the 'hard edges' of the mesomorphic body are achieved through exercise and competition which takes it outside of social context, the 'soft edges' of the endomorphic body are acquired within social contexts. These 'soft edges' threaten masculine self-identification in a number of ways. First, and more usually, a person's appearance may suggest that they are older than they actually are. This does not refer to the 'mutton dressed as lamb' spectacle, where Fairhurst (1998) has described how the older women in her study tried carefully to alter their appearance in ways that were not out of kilter with ageing bodies. Second, putting on weight and loss of muscle tone can sometimes result in a hairy chest with pendulous breasts to complement the 'gut-bucket' that is only just covered by a tee-shirt several sizes too small. Whilst the endomorphic individual is not felt to ignore everyday social roles and obligations, he was often critically regarded as having developed through overeating, regular binge drinking, and occasionally smoking, an impaired ability to meet the everyday demands of lived male identity. Finally, in comparison to the mesomorph in whom the definition of and concern with the body is central, the endomorph is perceived to indulge in excessive appetites whilst ignoring the presentational demise of male gender identity.

The ectomorph (tall and thin) only occasionally appeared as an explicit body shape in informant accounts of healthy and unhealthy others – specifically, in the guise of the marathon runners known to one informant. In this context, the training to acquire the stamina to run marathons contained features that informants felt were unhealthy with respect to the mesomorphic individual. In particular, one participant observed that the discipline of running every day left barely enough energy in a colleague to teach – to the extent that this colleague regularly fell asleep during his lunch break and went to bed mid-evening. Similarly, perceived imbalances in food intake – for example, high calorific bingeing in the build-up to a race – were felt to contribute to a state of artificial fitness.

Interestingly, whilst the endomorphic shape was perceived to distort and blur external physical gender definitions, the process of defining mesomorphic and ectomorphic shapes was felt, in certain circumstances such as weightlifting and marathon running, to distort and harm internal body structures. This was felt to be done by the altering of 'natural shapes and postures' which then constricted the locations of and spaces for internal organs, blood supply and nerve routes. Such constriction was felt to 'put pressure' on internal body structures, causing them to operate on the boundary between performance and breakdown.

A final but crucial point to make is that none of the informants used anything but vague shape descriptors of healthy others. The healthy body, as opposed to health-promoting behaviours, was far less substantially defined than unhealthy bodies. The importance of this point in relation to the evaluation of one's own health is further developed in considering the 'pragmatic mode of embodiment' and the final subsidiary category of 'evaluating social fitness'.

Pragmatic embodiment

For most participants this was the key level of embodiment irrespective of their own health-related behaviours. The interview transcripts represent, more than anything else, explanatory accounts of being healthy and male in the context of having a 'normal everyday body'. This is the primary mode of agency in the social world for the men in this study. It is not a presentational mode of construction which categorizes according to body shape, but rather a functional mode of construction categorized according to socially ordered and ordering male gender roles ('father', husband', 'brother', 'uncle', 'grandfather', 'mate' and 'worker').

For most of the informants investment in a pragmatic embodiment (the immediate everyday social body) involved the 'losing' or marginalization of the physical body as a primary mode for experiencing the social world. 'Fitting in' with regard to the pragmatic body marks the collectivization and domination of the individual embodied actor by the imperatives of gendered role practices. The praxis of 'father', 'husband' and 'worker' is the means by which the individual's masculinity and health is socially affirmed. In this sense the pragmatic body may be where, in Bourdieu's terms, informants fulfil the demands of their habitus. To be both male and 'functionally fit' is a measure of the degree to which one is or has 'social fit'. In this respect, it is suggested that the pragmatic body is the primary site for interaction between social structure and practice. For it is in the pragmatic body that the daily problems of gender affirmation and power are played out (Heller 1984).

Experiential embodiment

In some respects experiential embodiment is the most problematic level of male embodiment for health professionals. In its spaces the social and physical boundaries touch. It is suggested that the experiential body is the primary site for the experience of emotion, in the sense of experiencing 'well-being' or saying that you 'feel good' when someone asks you how you are. That said, since it was physical body experience that was the focus of this study, one would have to look to the work of others (Lakoff 1987; Freund 1990; Lupton 1998) to justify such an assertion. For example, Freund (1990: 453) has argued that 'emotions represent a juncture between society and the most personal realms of an individual's experiences'.

In terms of the physical body, informants generally experienced their bodies in a fragmented and contentious manner. Physical experience, such as the 'blood tingling' after a good physical workout, represented fleeting moments of conscious experience of hidden visceral processes. One informant, in talking about why he exercises, seems to imply that one may desire to reach a degree of focus in exercise whereby the social pragmatic body is temporarily bracketed out of perception. More often, it is the physical body which for these men is rarely known or experienced in totality. A broken leg, sinus infection, a pulled muscle, these are fragmented and flickering bodily (and emotional?) intrusions into the social locations of pragmatic embodiment. Responses to such bodily intrusions may, in themselves, represent affirmation of a pragmatic gendered embodiment. It appears to be only in the context of acute (e.g. brain tumour, heart attack) or chronic illness and disability (e.g. diabetes) that the visceral body penetrates both the levels of pragmatic and experiential embodiment to constrain the social self.

Visceral embodiment

If the normative, pragmatic and experiential levels of embodiment are variously the locations of an individual's social identity, then visceral embodiment, for these informants, furnishes an indirect – in the sense of not being consciously experienced – grounding with the natural cosmos. Visceral embodiment is one of the depths that cannot be perceived by others or the self except when it surfaces through the experiential body or when it becomes the object of invasive medical observation or treatment. For most informants it is the one level of embodiment that is prior to the social world, endowing the individual with a particular genetic inheritance derived from the general species and its particular biological progenitors: 'the body you're born with'.

This is not to argue a kind of genetic determinism. Participant discourse might speak of health-promoting behaviours, such as exercise or weight control, having the ability to alter body shape and improve certain biological processes such as respiratory function or cardiovascular efficiency. Reference was made to genetic endowment influencing one's potential for 'taking a heart attack' or 'getting cancer', conditions which could develop irrespective of presentational and functional (ill) health implicit in the normative and pragmatic levels of embodiment. At a more prosaic level, one informant, when asked 'How do you get a healthy body?', responded:

> *Interviewee (I)*: It is just basically within your genes. But obviously, how long you live and the activities you create from that obviously help. You are either born with it or you are not born with it.
> *Researcher (R)*: Genes are an important factor?
> *I*: It's a wee bit like losing your hair. There is nothing you can do about it. Some people are going to go bald, some aren't. I'm quite sure if they did a clinical study on it there would be certain types of lifestyle that would keep your hair a wee bit longer. Like growing old. You can do anything you like to stay young but at the end of the day you are going to get old.
>
> (Quantity surveyor, 37)

What this informant appears to be saying is that adopting a particular lifestyle, or set of behaviours, as a strategy to improve some facet of the self, does not significantly override underlying biological imperatives. In this sense, the social construction of 'healthy bodies' is not perceived to intrude into or structure this level of embodiment.

However, the common notion that the body 'puts itself in order' or 'fixes itself' points to the presence and operation of a generalized background process of 'body maintenance' which acts with the social levels of presentational and functional health to promote a sense of consonance in health. The processes of 'body maintenance' are, as the informants acknowledge, subject to the impact of injury (at work or through sport), illness and ageing. These are seen to impair the ability of the body to effect a recovery of sufficiency in functional terms. It is in this context that, for example, a strained shoulder muscle may be perceived to have a lower level of resistance to strain than one not strained.

The notion of body maintenance also encompasses a view that its processes are prescient, in the sense of conducting surveillance of the application of the pragmatic body to routine everyday tasks and, more importantly, to more spontaneous exertion. Thus, informants talk of the body warning you if you 'attempt to exceed its capabilities'. For example, one informant, when on holiday, decided to climb Schiehallion, one of the Scottish Munros situated in the Grampian Mountain range. He reached the top but his legs ached and he was so 'out of puff' that he felt his body was telling him that he had reached his (the body's) limit. More prosaically, taking part in a game of football, having last played at school 15 years previously, was, for a couple of the informants, motivated by an enthusiastic sense of 'once learnt, never forgotten' – never mind that physically the body may not be up to a full game, and stopping after a while with breathing laboured and tee-shirt soaked with sweat. To recall the words of one informant cited in the previous chapter:

> The things you did before with the greatest of ease are now not so easy.
>
> (Quantity surveyor, 37)

Managing ambiguity

The previous category says something about the way in which informants perceive, compose and experience embodiment in the context of everyday life. In a gendered health context, the management of embodiment is a practical problem. A curious aspect of the previous category is the degree to which informants resist the prevailing cultural equation of presentation (mesomorph) = masculine = health. Resolving the apparent incompatibility of the cultural exposition of this equation with the felt immediacies of a 'normal everyday body' – function = masculine = 'fitness' – is an exercise in 'managing ambiguity'.

Analysis of informant accounts reveals two main elements to this exercise. The first of these elements is found in informant descriptions of healthy others. Upon reflection, these descriptions were generally full of behavioural content but surprisingly non-committal when it came to body shape, beyond statements such as 'he had a tidy look about him' or 'he'll be the right weight for his height'. In presentational terms, the healthy body is never really substantiated by informants. It is almost an abstract concept. This may leave it more accessible to self-identification by the informant in public forms of discourse such as that involved in epidemiological and general practice surveillance.

Of itself this would not be sufficient to explain how informants could transpose the everyday function = masculine = fitness equation into the discourses of health promotion and primary care screening. 'I do my job OK' or 'I take the kids swimming' are not measures of the surveillance of individual health. In effect, there remains for informants the problem of how to deal with a reflexive application of precisely the kind of classificatory assessment that they make in defining healthy and unhealthy (male) individuals – behaviour(s) = form = (un)healthy = (change behaviour). Essentially, the embodied self-image of the pragmatic body is that of a presentational alter ego, a younger 'naturally healthy' body – me, as I was 'as a kid', 'before I got married', 'before I became a dad and gave up football'. This body is neither mesomorphic nor endomorphic. As such, it can be aligned across the domains of body schema – normatively with the healthy other which is given as a generalizable and, hence, open definition available to appropriation, and pragmatically with the functional self.

Evaluating social fit-ness

Evaluating the health of others is confined almost exclusively, among informants, to the presentational mode of construction. This process has been described in the context of the category 'male body schema' and alluded to in the preceding category 'managing ambiguity'. Perhaps the key element for health educators and others to consider, within the concept of 'being in shape', is how informants evaluate, in health and gender terms, their own forms of projected embodiment.

'Evaluating social fit-ness' refers to the basis on which that evaluation is made. Social fit-ness can be defined as the degree to which an individual is able to sustain a consonance, or 'fit', between the achievement of everyday gendered tasks and the sufficiency of physical fitness that is required to realize those tasks. Most informants conceptualized health as fitness but were clear that they meant more than physical fitness (see the discussion of this concept in the preceding chapter). Indeed, 'fitness' seemed to have more relevance or significance than 'health', with some informants feeling that the two terms were interchangeable but tending to favour the use of the former: 'being fit', 'feeling fit', 'you should be fit enough to cope', 'feel reasonably fit', 'keep fit' and 'fitness is for a purpose'. To be able to go to work, play with the kids, put up an extension or play football was generally felt to require 'sufficient' fitness rather than an excess of it. You are fit for what you have to do. In this sense, fitness is contingent upon the individual, and thus the infinitely variable construction and interpretation of everyday gendered roles and obligations. These processes of construction and interpretation are, in turn, mediated by the intrusion or absence of the experiential – and, by implication, the visceral – body into the social spaces of the pragmatic body.

Summary

In describing and then interpreting the range of cultural notions about male bodies and health, one can perceive how, in the everyday social contexts of those informants presented in this book, the concept of 'being in shape' offers a potential technology of individual affirmation grounded in the need to fulfil the demands of their pragmatic everyday embodiment. 'Being in shape' should not be taken to imply that the embodied individual is necessarily active in pursuing health as a body project. This would have been better represented by using the term *keeping* rather than *being*. Instead, as a concept it can be defined as the imperative to engage the demands of one's habitus from an embodied perspective. In this, the social practices of gender – grounded in narrative biography – may operate in a way that subverts that particular discourse of health education and political imperative that promotes personal responsibility for health. This possibility is explored in the case study of well man screening presented and analysed in the following chapter.

CHAPTER 6

PREVENTION
AND AGENCY

Preventive screening emerged as one of the key priorities of the National Health Service (NHS) in Scotland in the early 1990s (Scottish Office Home and Health Department 1989; Scottish Office Home and Health Department 1991; Scottish Office Department of Health 1992). This shift from the peripheral and patchy role that this activity had been given during the previous forty-odd years since the foundation of the NHS, was underpinned by several significant reports and papers that emerged towards the end of the 1980s. These

- identified Scotland as having the highest mortality rate from coronary heart disease for both men and women, in comparison with the rest of the world (General Registrar Office for Scotland 1989);
- identified a failure to provide an integrated CHD prevention programme in Scotland along the lines of *Heart Beat Wales* and *Look After Your Heart* (National Audit Office 1989);
- reported findings from the Scottish Heart Health Study which provided a national risk factor profile for Scotland (Tunstall-Pedoe *et al.* 1989);
- made recommendations for a national approach to the prevention of CHD that would adopt a dual intervention approach combining population-level health education with screening for high-risk groups (Working Group on Prevention and Health Promotion 1989);
- set national targets for the major CHD risk factors – smoking, diet in relation to obesity and blood pressure (Department of Health 1989).

A solution for increasing health education and preventive screening activity in respect of CHD and the other major preventable causes of mortality was provided by the introduction, in April 1990, of a new service contract for general medical practitioners. This contract required general practitioners to become active in health promotion by routinely screening all adults aged 16–74 registered with their practice every three years and providing health promotion as appropriate.

Well man clinics had begun to emerge in the late 1980s. Their appearance was prompted by the successful introduction of well woman clinics in primary care in the early 1980s. Early well man clinics were primarily concerned with screening for CHD risk factors in men aged 35 and over (Clements 1991), sexual health, physical and mental health, or a combination of all of these (Trevelyan 1989).

However, the introduction of the 1990 contract and the development of improved measures of risk for CHD (Shaper *et al.* 1986; Tunstall-Pedoe 1989) had two consequences which shaped the subsequent delivery and content of the clinic in this case study. First, the amount of time available for screening and lifestyle advice became restricted by the need to 'process' men through the clinic. One study observed that most practices would have to approach one in ten of men aged 46–65 on their practice lists to provide this service, even though the 1990 contract said that one consultation in three years was sufficient (Cook *et al.* 1990). In the case of the study clinic the doctor used to allow 30 minutes for each consultation, covering broader psychosocial issues such as the family, marriage, stress and potential sexual problems. But, as he commented prior to one of the consultations: 'We just couldn't get through the numbers at that rate so we gradually reduced it to, to hitting the target . . . points.' So around 15 minutes was allowed for each consultation. This meant that in a period of $2\frac{1}{2}$ hours the doctor could undertake ten consultations, though usually not all those invited could or wanted to attend. In effect, the 'target points' related primarily to the prevention of ischaemic heart disease.

Secondly, time constraints meant that the only feasible way to fulfil the health-promotion element was to adopt a straightforward information-giving approach, leaving it to the patient to decide whether to apply the knowledge imparted (verbally or in leaflets). The objectives for the well man clinic which is analysed in this chapter stated that:

> Once the patient has attended the clinic he should: be able to understand the benefit of a healthy lifestyle; have details of other agencies that can assist with identified problems, e.g. smoking clinic, dietary clinic; understand the principles of a healthy diet; know about safe alcohol limits; and understand the risk factors for ischaemic heart disease.

Implicit in this is a concern with achieving a particular preventive outcome: a reduction in morbidity and mortality due to ischaemic heart disease. In this respect, a second type of health-education approach underpins that of 'information giving' and 'patient choice'. 'Health education of this type operates within the medical model and is successful when appropriate behaviour change occurs' (Tones 1982: 2). In this context the *raison d'être* of health education becomes that of facilitating personal behaviour change. This is predicated upon two further assumptions: that individuals have a great deal of influence over their personal decisions and actions regarding diet, exercise and other lifestyle behaviours; and that changes in these personal behaviours can, in turn, significantly affect health outcomes (Davison *et al.* 1991).

In this scenario, Vaskilampi (1981: 193) notes the counter-argument, promulgated by critics such as Illich, to a medically directed health education:

> In health education, medical professionals define the values and norms of behaviour: that which is healthy is good, and that which is unhealthy is bad. Thus the medical profession is an agent of social control in everyday life.

The clinic as cultural event

The application of the core analytical category 'being in shape', to an analysis of the case-study data (interview transcripts and fieldnotes) can be seen, at one level, as an exercise in verifying and demonstrating the relevance of this analytical category. This is achieved by regrounding it in empirical data collected as part of the study but not considered when exploring cultural notions of the male body and health in the previous chapters. At another level, it is as one considers the temporal structure of the clinic in conjunction with its physical dimensions and interaction between the actors that the 'space' of the clinic comes alive as a cultural event. In doing so it becomes accessible to analysis and interpretation using the concept 'being in shape'. In the analytical interpretation that follows one sees the clinic, from the patient's perspective, as an event in which the patient, moving between different domains of embodiment, is never quite enmeshed in a Foucauldian public health/health-promotion discourse aimed at constructing and controlling 'healthy bodies'.

Spatial and temporal dimensions of the clinic

The space in which this interaction between doctor and patient took place was a room, rectangular in shape and measuring about 17 feet by 12 feet. In the top corner of the room, on the same side as the patients' entrance, was the doctor's desk. The desk faced the wall. However, the first physical object that the patient met was a chair situated at the end of the desk. The doctor's chair was usually swivelled towards him. Only a corner of the desk separated them. Beyond the doctor, on the far wall, was a window. The blinds were normally down but open. Along the wall opposite the desk were a sink unit, worktop and cupboards, the rest of the wall being taken up by an examination couch. A curtain on a running rail, fitted to the ceiling, allowed the doctor to screen off the couch from the rest of the room when a physical examination was in process. The head of the couch almost touched the wall in which the door was situated. On that same wall, but beyond the area that could be screened off, was a height measure fixed to the wall, and below it was a set of scales.

The case-study clinic employed a shortened consultation. This consultation had two components. The first involved 'taking a history'. According to the clinic protocol, this included, as appropriate, a history of diet, smoking, exercise, alcohol, drugs, allergies, occupation, family history and immunization status. Descriptions of the temporal structure of the clinic are taken from fieldnotes, recorded by the researcher when observing a series of five clinic sessions (November 1991 and January 1992), and transcripts of interviews conducted with informants within a week of their attendance, or otherwise, at the well man clinic. The following extract from fieldnotes illustrates how this protocol only loosely guided the interaction between patient and doctor:

06/12/91: 0845, 2nd consultation

The doctor goes out to find the next appointment and reappears shortly afterwards ushering in the second 'customer' of the morning. This man is wearing a black leather jacket, jeans and trainers. He glances at me as he sits down. This is noticed by the doctor who introduces me as a 'young doctor' and instructs the man to 'just forget all about him'. The doctor has sat down and is reading some notes on the desk in front of him. The 'patient' glances at the notes that the doctor is reading, (assuming that they are his medical notes?).

History: The doctor begins this session by checking out the 'patient's' family history. Both parents are dead. He's now an ex-smoker. Used to be a forty-a-day person but stopped in the summer of 1990. The 'patient' is on medication for a reflux problem that was diagnosed in 1990. He has had broken arms a couple of times. Had a history of headaches that stopped around the time he stopped smoking. During this exchange the patient and the doctor are not looking at each other. The doctor asks him about his diet. The patient replies 'Not particularly'. (Maybe he misunderstood the question.) The doctor persists and asks him how often he eats fried food. Both are looking at each other now, smiling. No regular exercise. Doesn't drink much alcohol. He's a project engineer. Works offshore. Has two children. Had a tetanus booster a week ago. The doctor explains about the length of the booster. The doctor indicates that he is now going to do some checks and then send him along to the nurse to take some blood. He then asks the patient for the urine sample that he was requested to provide.

A physical examination and measurement of height, weight and blood pressure then followed the history. Investigations included urinalysis and optional measurement of serum glucose and cholesterol (initially non-fasting). The clinic had a written protocol which included guidance on 'indications for cholesterol measurement' and a treatment protocol for hypercholesterolaemia. The account of the examination that follows is taken from the same observation as the history used above:

> *Examination*: The patient is asked to step behind the curtain which is partially drawn, and strip down to his underpants. While the patient is doing this the doctor is over at the sink conducting a urinalysis. The doctor approaches the patient. He now has a stethoscope around his neck. He is talking about the weather and asks the patient to lie on the couch. The patient lies down and stares at the ceiling. The doctor checks, in order: eyes, neck, pulse, stethoscope to chest (doctor now leaning over patient, speaking in low voice about work), stomach (patient reassured that 'things are fine, great'), blood pressure, patient asked to sit forward and take deep breaths (doctor says 'good'), pats shoulder. Patient asked to slip onto the scales and then stand against the wall for height measurement. Patient told to slip his things back on. Doctor returns to his desk, sits down and starts writing in the patient's notes. Patient gets dressed and is directed to the nurse treatment room for a blood test. The patient leaves smiling.

All the consultations that were observed had the same basic structure as the one above, although within the 'taking a history' or 'examination' components the ordering of that component could vary, as could the nature and content of the interaction between patient and doctor. Given that all the consultations shared certain basic structural elements it is possible to represent the consultation diagramatically (Figure 6.1). In turn, it is the spatial and temporal ordering of the clinic that is represented in this diagram that becomes the starting point for a cultural interpretation of the clinic using the analytical concept 'being in shape'.

Embodied experience of the clinic

Spatially and temporally, the clinic is divided into three areas. Two of these, around the desk and the examination couch, are zones of embodiment,

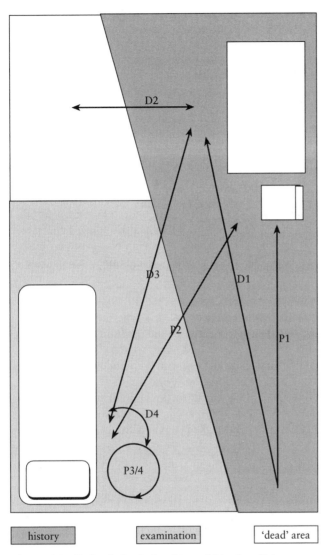

Figure 6.1 Embodied relationships within the clinic

whilst the area in the top left of the diagram contains a sink and is a neutral 'dead' space used by the doctor to allow the patient to make his initial transition between the two zones of embodiment. The area around the desk which both patient (P1) and doctor (D1) enter together, from the clinician's perspective, operates on two levels. The first of these is overtly medical – family history, allergies, immunization status, urinalysis. Its focus is the *visceral* body of the patient and its purpose is acquiring or confirming knowledge relating to that person's physical state. This is a medical discourse which the patient contributes to but does not influence. During this phase of interaction between doctor and patient, the two rarely engaged in eye contact. In fact, during the 'history' quoted above, the patient appeared to 'miss' the switch from clinical to risk discourse and the doctor had to repeat his question about diet. At a second level is the discourse of risk referred to by Lupton (1993), in which the patient is probed regarding certain prespecified health-related behaviours: smoking, exercise, diet, alcohol and drugs. This is a discourse that clearly the patient is more familiar with and, to an extent, engages in. The cues between doctor and patient become more frequent: eye contact, smiling, jokes. From the patient's perspective this discourse is not so much about the *visceral* body as it is about a *normative* presentational body. It is a public dialogue focused on parallel lay and medical constructions of healthy and unhealthy images that were discussed in Chapter 3. An impression that came from observing a number of similar consultations was that doctor and patient appear to collude in the playing out of this dialogue. In the following excerpt a diabetic informant recalls:

> I suppose when I, I said I didn't drink, 'cause at the moment I don't drink . . . I never do. But then it occurred to me . . . hold on a minute. I had a gin last night because . . . I'd had such a hard day at work, I thought, well it was the first time in 3 months . . . since Christmas in fact, I can have a drink and Fran and I both had a gin. Then I thought, here's me saying I'd none . . . he's going to do a blood test. It's probably full of alcohol. I'd better say 'Oh well, the occasional one'. But em . . . no. He didn't bat an eyelid right the way through all the questions. Which I thought was quite good cause it was just a mechanical yes, no, yes, no.
>
> (Technical design manager, 37)

In this sense, the parameters of the consultation are familiar and unchallenging. The two actors, fully clothed, engage in a discourse in which the shape of the body is never articulated in relation to the self. The critical implication of this disjuncture between a social risk discourse and consideration of the personal body becomes clearer by looking at the nature of embodiment encountered in area around the examination couch (bottom left of Figure 6.1).

Before analysing this area as a zone of embodiment, it is important to discern how the spatial and temporal interaction between doctor and patient facilitates transition between states of embodiment. As the doctor finishes taking the history he directs the patient's attention to the couch and essentially offers a physical examination to the patient. For some this was unexpected. Having described how the doctor took his history, this informant goes on to say:

Em after, that took about 5, only about 5 minutes, I would say, and then he explained that he was going to do, em, just give us the once over. Sort of examine us, em, and he asked us to go to one side and strip off to me underwear. Em that, that took us a little bit by surprise as I say because I was, even at the beginning of the, of the session it was going at, more or less as I had expected.

(Mechanical engineer, 37)

When the patient walks toward the couch (P2) the doctor does not accompany him. Instead, he takes the patient's urine sample to the sink unit (D2), where he conducts a quick urinalysis. Whilst this is happening, the patient has reached the couch and proceeds to undress. The doctor returns to the desk and writes down the result of the urinalysis in the patient's notes. He then follows the patient to the examination couch (D3). At this point the patient has either lain down on the couch or is waiting for an invitation to do so from the doctor. If an invitation to lie down has to be made the doctor will usually do so whilst still at his desk. Importantly, the doctor does not 'enter' or 'cross over' into another spatial domain at the same time as the patient. As will be shown, this is important because the two domains represent qualitatively different states of embodiment from the patient's perspective. The patient constructs the area of the examination couch in terms of his personal *experiential* embodiment, rather than of the social *normative* embodiment he experiences at the desk. During the consultation the patient enters the spatial domain of his own personal experiential self before the doctor. In a sense, he establishes the examination couch as the site of his subjective self prior to the doctor's arrival to conduct the examination. The examination then begins.

06/12/91: 0955, 5th consultation

Examination: Doctor at sink doing urinalysis. Patient stripping behind the drawn curtain. Doctor picks up his stethoscope, pulls the screen partly back and tells the patient that he'll take his height and weight first. As the patient stands against the wall he appears to be pushing his shoulders back (trying to maximize his shoulder spread?). The patient lies down on couch. Looks at ceiling. Doctor using stethoscope to examine patient's chest. Feels stomach then ankles (peripheral pulse?). Patient sits up. Doctor asks for deep breaths and takes soundings using the stethoscope on the patient's back. Patient avoiding eye contact with the doctor. Patient lies down. Doctor checks blood pressure (reassures patient that 'everything is fine'). Patient points out knot at back of knee. Doctor reassures that this will settle down. The skin is loose and this will help haema? to develop. Injury result of being hit by a hockey stick. Patient told to get dressed. Told that he 'seems to be in good shape'. Patient pats stomach and says 'apart from this'. Doctor tells him to lose half a stone. Patient leaves at 1012.

Interestingly, in the above example the doctor starts the examination by measuring the patient's height and weight (P3/4, D4). During this process the patient attempts to present himself so as to maximize shoulder spread and pull in his stomach. This is only temporary, and posture soon reverts to what is usual for the patient. However, during this short time, the patient seems to be aware of his body as an object of scrutiny and so he attempts to adopt, or mimic, a more defined (mesomorphic?) body shape. As discussed in Chapter 3, height and weight are integral components of informants' descriptions of healthy others. Therefore, mimicking may indicate that, although the patient is engaged in a primarily experiential mode of embodiment, he recognizes and responds to a procedure that is part of risk factor discourse and thereby switches, momentarily, into a normative presentational mode. This indicates that modes of embodiment do not necessarily have to be spatially defined. It also indicates something of the indeterminate nature of embodiment, that is, of the perceptually contingent nature of modes of embodiment, discussed earlier in the previous chapter.

Informant accounts support the view, though, that this phase of the consultation is primarily concerned with the experiential body as its point of departure. This and the following example further illustrate the fragmentary nature of this experiential embodiment:

> At that point I asked him about, I've got a varicose vein on my right leg, at the back. Em, I said while he was examining us, can I just ask you for your comments on this vein because it's, it's something that I've once asked the doctor about previously and, eh, I feel it's, for a start it's ugly. Em, and also it's starting to give us a little bit of pain, not very much but I'm aware that it's there now. In the past I haven't been. And he was quite sort of em, nonchalant about it really. He said, oh it's not a problem, he said we'll have it, surgery done on it.
>
> (Mechanical engineer, 37)

This informant mentioned his varicose vein for two reasons. First, his body is unclothed, giving the doctor 'access' to the problem and the patient an opportunity for bringing it to the doctor's attention. Second, the pain that the patient has been experiencing coincides with his visit to the clinic. It is uppermost in his mind and the examination offers the chance to seek a solution. By contrast, another informant, when interviewed in the week after his going to the clinic, was asked if there had been anything he had wanted to raise but had not:

> There was one thing that I actually completely forgot . . . and it's been going on for years. Eh, I can get short of breath. You know, just sitting speaking just now. I often get a deep breath you know, and I sometimes have problems catching my breath.
>
> (Drilling equipment salesman, 38)

This problem had not been experienced by the informant immediately before or during his visit to the clinic so he forgot to raise it. For the informant this was compounded by the nature of his experience of the problem. That is, the shortness of breath was, for him, an everyday phenomenon, almost taken for granted and thus less noticeable than the varicose vein experienced by the previous informant.

The experiential body is thus the site of the examination. During this procedure the patient does not 'detach' himself from his experience of his body in the present. He continues to experience his body and the working of the doctor over it. But at the same time he adopts strategies that allow the doctor access to this subjective self. In the extracts from fieldnotes that have been cited previously in connection with the examination, the patient again avoids eye contact with the doctor. He looks at the ceiling, anywhere but at his own body. It is only if the patient has a particular problem, such as a varicose vein, or a cyst at the back of his knee, that he will draw the doctor's attention to a specific site on his body. The strategies adopted by the patient which contribute to controlling the intimate nature of the inter-action between same-sex bodies should not be taken to imply a detaching of the social self from the physical self. This is described very well in the following extract:

> *Interviewee (I)*: I tend to become very passive in these situations and just relax as much as possible. In the doctor's or in the dentist. I try and make a conscious effort to relax and just, but on the other hand, try . . . you know, try and be aware of what's going on. I don't sort of become totally detached from it.
>
> *Researcher (R)*: Why do you try and relax? Be passive?
>
> I: I think it's nice when you're stretched out. I just don't get the chance to do that during the day, to crash out. And that sort of thing probably. I probably think it makes his job easier.
>
> R: Right.
>
> I: Em . . . to see that I'm not tense about the situation and also I'm not particularly interested in, in what he's doing in a critical sort of way.
>
> R: Right.
>
> I: So . . . he can get on with his job without worrying too much about me thinking he's got to talk to me for example, throughout, which he might feel that he has to do . . . to keep up some kind of rapport.
>
> (Solicitor, 39)

The patient manages the encounter by locating himself at the margins of this domain of embodiment, leaving the main spaces of the domain of the experiential body to the doctor. What this last account also illustrates is that the doctor's attempt to manage the encounter by keeping up a (*sotto voce*) reassuring banter with the patient may be unnecessary from the patient's perspective. Nevertheless, it may be important for the doctor in allowing

him to manage the boundaries of his own interaction with the patient.
Young (1989) and Lawler (1991) have previously commented on the use of
various verbal, non-verbal and visual techniques employed by nurses and
doctors to 'manage' such intimate moments in a clinical encounter.

The purpose of the examination, as the patient perceives it, is for the
doctor to be able to explore the health of the visceral body through
the boundary of the experiential body. This perception of the purpose of
the doctor's actions has consistency within the cosmology of male body
schema, in that, in the first phase of the consultation – 'taking a history' –
the doctor seeks access to the visceral body through the mediating boundary of the normative body. The purpose of the clinic is thus experienced
by the patient as an underlying concern with the visceral body, a domain
of embodiment that is taken for granted because of its location beneath the
surface of the body – out of sight. Equally, it is a domain to which the
doctor is perceived to have access with the techniques of clinical medicine.
Some informants, however, expressed scepticism about the ability of the
doctor to perceive the visceral body in this way, without the help of invasive technology:

> Somebody could listen to your chest and you could be riddled with
> cancer, you know what I mean. They wouldn't know. You know there's
> a lot of things can't be detected just by a physical examination. You
> could have a mental disease . . . I suppose it gives them a rough outline
> but, em . . . I think unless you're actually doing tests and stuff like that,
> then it can't really be a proper picture of somebody's health.
>
> (Electrician, 34)

Once the examination is completed and height and weight have been
measured, the doctor crosses once more to his desk (D3) where, with his
back to the patient, who is putting his clothes back on, he makes some
further notes in the patient's file. In his turn, the patient returns to his chair
by the desk, making the transition from experiential to normative embodiment (P2). At this point most of the informants who attended the clinic
expected a more personal discourse to continue, one that would be directly
relevant to them this time instead of the formal, almost ritualistic, nature of
the preceding medical history and lifestyle review. But usually the doctor's
next words ensured that the opportunity to develop a personal discourse,
made available by the negotiated access to the personal levels of embodiment through the examination, was not followed through:

> He just said 'You're fine'. I wasn't told what my blood pressure was or
> told it was normal for my age and weight or whatever.
>
> (Accountant, 40)

> Didn't really get any information from it and nobody tells you why
> they are doing what they are doing. They don't show you a chart to

say this is your BP and this is the normal distribution of men in your
age group . . . you're within that.

(Industrial chemist, 38)

Instead, the patient is directed to the treatment room nurse, who will take a
couple of blood samples, with the assurance that they will be contacted if
the tests show elevated serum glucose or cholesterol levels.

Risk discourse and agency

It has been argued that change is not about choice. It is about taking
personal responsibility for one's health. By logical inference, health 'risks'
become self-imposed when behaviour is not modified. The 'victim' is to
blame. Crawford (1977: 678) has argued that increasing disenchantment
with the limits and costs of medicine weakened the 'traditional social control function of individualising disease through the biological model'. Instead,
the emergence of a social and political climate emphasizing self-help and
individual control over health (Illich 1976) opened the way to an ideology of
individual responsibility which 'poses an alternate social control formula-
tion. It replaces reliance on therapeutic intervention with a behavioural
model which only requires good living' (Crawford 1977: 678).

More recently, in examining the functions of risk discourse in public
health, Lupton (1993: 432–3) has argued that

> Health education emphasizing risks is a form of pedagogy, which, like
> other forms, serves to legitimate ideologies and social practices. Risk
> discourse in the public health sphere allows the state, as the owner
> of knowledge, to exert power over the bodies of its citizens. Risk dis-
> course, therefore, especially when it emphasizes lifestyle risks, serves as
> an effective Foucaldian agent of surveillance and control that is diffi-
> cult to challenge because of its manifest benevolent goal of maintaining
> standards of health.

Similarly, Armstrong (1983), writing about medical knowledge in Britain
in the twentieth century, has extended and aligned Foucault's ideas about
the surveillance and control of bodies to the post-war emergence of several
medical disciplines, including general practice. In these terms, the general
practice contract and policy statements on health education and CHD prevention can be interpreted as reinforcing general practice as an institutionalized mechanism of surveillance in which risk discourse, and hence
the control of bodies, is paramount.

Analysis of the case study illustrates, however, that an interpretation
based entirely on an imperative to surveillance and the control of bodies
through risk discourse is overly simplistic. In terms of a power/knowledge

analysis of the clinic, this approach is problematic since it comes to represent, in Silverman's (1987: 191) words 'a spurious discourse of truth'. This
is not to argue that it is not a legitimate discourse, simply to say that it
should not 'close off' the observer from consideration of the existence and
impact of other discourses. In this instance, it fails to take account of a lay
discourse of embodiment and the degree to which the temporal-spatial structure of the clinic colludes in sustaining elements of that lay discourse on
male embodiment and health. Indeed, Foucault (1988: 19) is himself cited
on the need to look for other discourses when he comments in a later essay
that

> perhaps I've insisted too much on the technology of domination and
> power. I am more and more interested in the interaction between one-
> self and others and in the technologies of individual domination, the
> history of how an individual acts upon himself, in the technology of
> self.

Figure 6.2 summarizes the organization of the well man clinic from the
perspective of the analytical concept of 'being in shape' (Figure 5.1). The key
relationships in this analytical interpretation serve to underline the explanatory power of a discourse of embodiment. In turn, one is led to question
the efficacy of an ideology of personal responsibility for health grounded in
a discourse of risk with the goal of 'constructing healthy bodies'.

This critique is explicated through consideration of the principal interrelationships represented in Figure 6.2. These, in turn, focus on the concepts
of 'personal responsibility' and 'constructing healthy bodies'. As has been
discussed previously, the clinic's focus is on the relationship between three
modes of embodiment – normative, experiential, visceral – represented by
the relationship A-B-C. In this relationship, the patient's perspective is that
the doctor seeks to access the visceral body via the normative body (taking
a history/risk discourse) and later, via the experiential body (examination).
The spatial-temporal structuring of the clinic means that the normative
social body (A) is separated out and away from the experiential individual
body (B) so that the individual self never becomes exposed to a public
health discourse of risk.

A second effect of the focus on (C) via (A) and (B) is that the doctor misses
an opportunity to individualize and thereby insert a critical and potentially
reflective juncture of the normative healthy body and the experiential body
of the individual. In this way the experience of the clinic does not challenge
the pragmatic biographical basis of the normative image by which the individual perceives himself in terms of his public 'health persona', a notion
initially referred to in Chapter 4.

That this does not occur is because, crucially, risk discourse does not allow
for an exploration of an individual's pragmatic mode of embodiment. This
is important because, as has been demonstrated previously, it is through

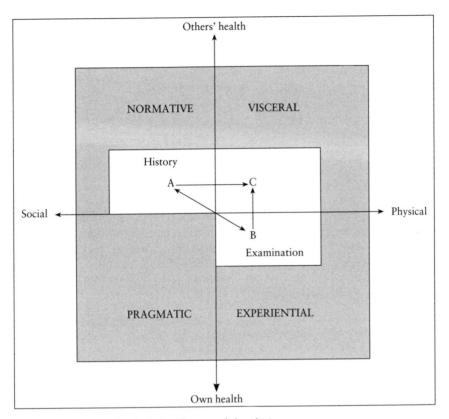

Figure 6.2 The embodied significance of the clinic

the pragmatic mode of everyday embodiment that personal responsibility is constructed and reconstructed. Of all his modes of embodiment, the pragmatic mode is the male's primary mode of insertion and agency in the social world.

It might thus be argued that the 'screening' of a normative male body compliant and accessible to the clinical 'gaze' becomes a singularly inappropriate and irrelevant task of the primary care professional. Is it then possible to turn that clinical gaze to the pragmatic body? The possibility is raised by one informant who, feeling that his expectations of the clinic had not been met, was asked what he felt should have occurred:

> Well . . . perhaps I mean a bit of exercise. Standing up and down off a seat or something and seeing how long it took you to get back to your normal resting rate or something like that. I mean a test of basic fitness really. I mean, I don't think you can tell how fit someone is just by looking them over and listening to their heartbeat.
>
> (Communications supervisor, 33)

The problem with seeing the measurement of physical fitness as a way forward for meaningful primary care screening of the well man is that fitness as a concept is primarily bound up with notions of the pragmatic everyday body and with the equation function = masculine = fitness (see Chapters 3 and 5). In this, having sufficient fitness is a personal and highly individual standard maintained within the social context of a web of interaction between social structure and gendered practices. That is, pragmatic embodiment cannot be extracted from its subjective social location.

Summary

In this sense, the temporal-spatial structuring of the well man clinic observed in this research engages most informants in responding to their normative, experiential and visceral modes of embodiment. However, it critically fails, or appears unable, to facilitate a coming together of the public health discourses of risk and healthy lifestyles within the parameters of the pragmatic embodiment of the individual.

CHAPTER 7

MEN'S HEALTH: SOME CONCLUSIONS

It is somewhat ironic that as this manuscript was being completed, the daily newspapers provided a depressing but apposite view of the state of sexual politics. Both tabloids and broadsheets were covering the UK government's latest initiative to promote the role of women in society. At the same time, a new campaign to help battered women was launched. This led to the juxtaposition of headlines such as 'Big Sister plans to boost teenagers' (*The Independent*, 10 November 1998) and 'WAR ON THE EVIL FATHERS' (*Scottish Express*, 10 November 1998). Meanwhile, an inside feature in the *Scottish Express* was saying that divorced (middle-class) fathers could be 'as good as any mother'.

In public health, where evidence-based work is increasingly considered an indispensable qualification for action, we rely on a partial and threadbare stock of evidence, which seems to mirror the good intentions but contradictory two-dimensional positions adopted by the fourth estate. Critically, we still know very little about how a baby boy will personally experience health over the course of his lifetime. Whilst men's health is a growing area of policy concern (Acheson 1998) it is also an area of study that, with exceptions, has been informed by some naïve and simplistic approaches. Men's health will continue to be sold short if we fail to bring to our work some understanding of the vibrancy, humour, complexity and morality of male experience to be found in lay knowledge. In that spirit, this book attempts to develop a more coherent analysis of men's health with special reference to embodied experience and health. It is an analysis that suggests that the impact of health and risk discourse on male experience is mediated and muted by the pragmatic demands of bodily engagement with the social world.

This book arrives at that conclusion through an assessment of a diverse range of evidence: theory, epidemiology, policy context, professional practice and lay knowledge. It is not easy to shape and develop an argument in this way, but it is a challenge for informed and evidence-based policy-making and practice. In doing so, the intention has been to avoid jumping between theoretical and empirical evidence in too precipitate a manner. To try and smooth out some of these connections, this concluding chapter considers some of the key learning points to be drawn from the evidence considered in the previous chapters.

Overall, the investigation of ideas about the social and cultural contexts of health, held by a particular group of men aged 30–40, demonstrates the extent to which informants' personal experiences of health are grounded in gendered perspectives of the body and of health. Analysis shows how the knowledge that informs their practice encompasses the interrelationships between men's concepts of the body and health and the biographical and social factors that informants use in organizing and maintaining their placement of the masculine 'self' within the context of everyday life. The issues that have emerged in the context of empirically based understanding of embodiment can only be said to apply to the informants, who were predominantly 'middle-class' and employed. Nevertheless, the subsequent analysis has implications for public health and health promotion that might be applicable to men of other ages and circumstances.

To start with, policy, professional practice and research are currently informed by inadequate conceptualization of the individual and notions of agency. Take this quote from the Department of Health's (1993) review of men's health:

> Despite an apparent indifference, if not resistance, to health promotion messages among men, it must be brought home to them that many of the risk factors to their health – such as smoking, physical inactivity, poor diet, excess alcohol consumption, unsafe sexual practices and risky behaviour likely to lead to accidents – are preventable. Thus the scope for men to improve their health, and to prolong active, healthy life, is considerable.

Health promotion does not pay attention to the lived experience of healthy or unhealthy bodies. What health promotion does is operate with an implicit theory of the body that is dissociated from everyday lived reality. The research presented here and elsewhere (Watson *et al.* 1996; Nettleton and Watson 1998b) provides a first step in developing theory explicitly located in embodied everyday experience. Health promotion is confronted with the conundrum that whilst it may promote particular prescriptions for a healthy life, it is what people do that counts.

Inasmuch as they are members of marginalized or disadvantaged groups, 'men' are being brought within the policy gaze, for example, in respect of current social inclusion initiatives such as welfare to work. As such, they have an identity that is related to the location of a given group within the structures of the prevailing socioeconomic system. Relatedly, white heterosexual middle-aged men are visible in the public health literature but relatively invisible in practice. This may be because they are often treated as a reference group against which other population groups are separated out for analysis. 'Men' turn up in practice with their identity and characteristics submerged beneath risk profiles and other anonomizing, but morally loaded, features of public health discourse. This holds across shifts in the policy agenda – from a neo-liberal ideology which privatizes health by devolving responsibility for managing risk to the individual (Petersen 1997: 194), to the new public health agenda which seeks to address the socioeconomic determinants of health in addition to the existing lifestyle focus. Both approaches to public health are driven by a moral imperative (Lupton 1995) and are underpinned by a set of more or less distinct values (WHO 1986, 1998a, 1998b; SODoH 1992, 1997; DoH 1992, 1998) which are considered appropriate in a democratic society. However, the ways in which different groups of men are located and thus realized within specific policy, practice and research contexts can be said to problematize and disregard notions of individual agency.

To take the available research evidence as an example, the *Leeds Declaration*, discussed in Chapter 3, was made on the basis that action to improve health could only become more effective if shortcomings in the existing epidemiological knowledge base of public health were addressed. Despite this, the literature on men's health is dominated by biological (differences between men and women, genetic makeup/the X chromosome, testosterone, sexual health, HIV/AIDS) and behavioural research. The latter assumes that individual men take risks and the main difference between men's and women's health is 'variations in exposure to risk factors' derived from forms of work and leisure activities. The two areas overlap, for example in the area of preventive screening, and both sit within a lifestyle view of health. Biology is important, but basically men's health is oriented around an individual framework of beliefs and behaviours (Lloyd 1996: 6). A smaller literature considers masculinity (the process of learning to be a man). However, the challenge to 'change, abandon or resist aspects of masculinity' (Sabo and Gordon 1995: 16) is problematic because it is presumed that all men benefit equally from being male in a patriarchal society and because masculinity is treated as a unitary construct. In this sense, the current literature generally fails to locate men's health within broader contemporary social and economic contexts and to recognize that a gender analysis needs to go beyond gender (Connell 1995).

Flowing from this point comes a second problem. As an explanation for health outcomes, masculinity is poorly understood and inadequately operationalized both within the practice and research communities. It has become orthodoxy among professionals and policy-makers to assume that men's susceptibility to ill health and disease is caused by the adoption and maintenance of lifestyles that are profoundly destructive of body and self. Changing such behaviours has thus become a preoccupation for health professionals. Such knowledge has informed a concern, particularly evident in professional nursing journals, to address deficits in men's health through the medium of innovative health-promotion initiatives (Darbyshire 1987; Trevelyan 1989; Jackson 1991; Fareed 1994; Robertson 1995). Working from a 'gender' perspective, that is, seeking to understand the gender basis of male lifestyles, thus becomes a preoccupation for health professionals as this quote from a nursing journal makes clear:

> Much ill-health among men is a consequence of lifestyle, and these are issues that nurses can address in their role as health educators. There is a need to help men recognise that stereotypical gender role behaviour . . . can pose a risk to health and could be changed.
>
> (Fareed 1994: 26)

Implicit in this perspective is a view that somehow poor health outcomes among men generally, and men in social class V especially, is a direct consequence of selfish, risky behaviour. This conclusion is reinforced by a moral assumption that such behaviour represents an abrogation of personal responsibility for health. This may reflect 'reality' for certain groups of men at particular points in the lifecourse. However, the concepts of health contained within informant accounts can be read differently. They suggest that such an abdication of personal responsibility to 'look after yourself' could be construed as altruistic gendered practice based around pragmatic interpretations of culturally appropriate scripts such as the 'breadwinner', the 'guardian' or the 'sturdy oak'.

A related question for professional agendas is whether the 'deficits' in men's health, so often reported in professional journals, are to be found in the attitudes, behaviour and values of men or whether they are to be found in the professional and ideological agendas that drive practice forward. Reading the many hours of interview transcripts for the present study, it is apparent that informants are aware of the main health-education messages relating to consumption of alcohol, eating, exercise, smoking, stress and weight control. Most would argue that, where possible, these messages have been practically translated into their everyday lives. They try and watch what they eat, they have cut down on the amount of alcohol they drink. Their accounts demonstrate use of the language that frames such messages both in conversation with the researcher and in the context of the well man clinic and of some of the concepts that underpin these messages. This might indicate that health educators have succeeded in creating a generic pool of concepts, terms and scripts which informants can call upon in situations such as the consultation or survey. What remains debatable is the extent to which the impetus for personal change derives from such knowledge or from changes in an individual's structural environment (work, family, community) and/or social practice (husband, worker, father) that may constrain or extend choice.

As such, this book does not offer solutions for those health professionals who try to promote men's health. In this sense, it does not show how to change men's health but it does suggest that those who are engaged in such enterprises need critically to reappraise their goals and expectations. Instead of arguing that men have to be educated to make better use of available resources – limited though those covering men's health 'issues' are – it is not certain that such resources adequately address issues relating to how men could maximize the ways in which they might respond to lifecourse transitions, a shifting civic values base or changes in social and economic structures.

Third, whilst social theorizing of the body has resulted in a restricted reading of the body, it can equally be argued that the risk/behaviour explanations that currently inform health promotion's interest in men's health are themselves the consequence of a restricted understanding of the central and defining influence of male embodiment. The data presented in previous chapters suggest that lay perspectives about embodiment underpin informants' health practices. This problematizes men's health for health promotion since the existence of such spaces, silences and confusions indicates the potential for choices and constraints other than those that are central to the promotion of healthy lifestyles. The core analytical category 'being in shape' illuminates an important tension between the promotion of personal responsibility for health and personal responsibility derived from the gendered and rather functional demands of pragmatic embodiment which ultimately constrain 'healthy choices'. Embodiment is thus an integrating concept that engages with the multilayered discourse and agendas around public health and health promotion.

What this suggests is that there is a need for research (full stop). Such research must be adequately theorized and methodologically sensitive. A recent men's health audit of 162 organizations covering NHS trusts, health boards, general practices, the voluntary sector and government agencies found that only 3 of the 81 respondents could identify and specify a research spend on men's health (Lloyd 1996). As Drever and Bunting (1997), among others, demonstrate, it is possible to subject existing data sets to an analysis of social class differences in health outcomes between different groups of men. However, this needs to be supported and 'fleshed out' by a comparative (intra-gender) social analysis of structural and power relations between hegemonic and subordinate/marginalized masculinities. In doing so it cannot be assumed that the characteristics of hegemonic masculinity are synonymous with social class I males and the features of subordinate masculinities with social class V males. The relevance of existing factors such as educational attainment and class or occupation should be examined since, of themselves, they may be insufficient as proxy indicators for differentiating between masculinities.

A particular challenge for policy-makers is suggested by some of the evidence in Chapter 1. Specifically, the evidence suggests that we are witnessing a more profound dislocation between young men in social class V and valued work opportunities, the family and civic society. This process has been recognized and forms one of the motivations behind the recent social inclusion initiatives. However, it remains an open question whether such action will engage equally with men and women and whether both will realize the benefits. Similarly, early assessment of interventions to build social capital suggests that developing and reinforcing social connectedness, trust and reciprocity within communities may benefit women but fail to engage men in those communities since the concept of social capital appears to privilege culturally female modes of exchange and support. Embodied practice crystallizes the choices and constraints that people face, particularly the interrelationship of structure and agency, and thus may be a useful conceptual window on how social capital is operationalized.

This moves us to a fifth and more theoretical set of issues, in that a problem for theorizing the body is to make coherent sense of this articulation. It could be argued that lay knowledge holds the conceptual keys to understanding the complex relationship between the body, self, culture and society. Lived experience is the articulation of these relationships. For example, in Chapter 3 informants acknowledge a prescribed version of the 'ideal body', yet in everyday practice resist, reject or find no personal meaning in such an ideal. The parameters of acceptance of and resistance to social structural constraints or cultural imperatives are drawn within lives that are highly contingent and variable, yet not infinitely self-determined. The body is individually experienced within the broad boundaries of existing, yet dynamic, structures. In this sense, any theorizing about the body should be grounded (Frank 1991). It is only in this way that we can avoid over-generalization generated from a theoretical focus at a structural or cultural level.

Relatedly, any theory needs to be dynamic. The data certainly suggest that culture, structure and people's embodied experiences are not static, for they change over time (for example, across the lifecourse). Similarly, as previous literature has shown, the body is not a unitary entity (Douglas 1982; Scheper-Hughes and Lock 1987) but can be conceptualized and understood as a set of relationships – for example – between the individual or social group and society. Identification of any similarity between individuals as socially grouped (for example, unemployed young men) and similarity across groups (for example, in resistance to the ideal body) will help further to make sense of these relationships.

Theory also needs to incorporate practical resistance to dominant views. In Chapter 4 it was suggested that any theorizing must not be over-deterministic, yet at the same time not ignore the physicality of the body. Both resistance to cultural norms and imagination in the face of structural constraints typify some of the accounts outlined previously. Embodied experiences challenge assumptions about personal responsibility for one's body or for one's health. For although some aspects of embodied experience are amenable to manipulation and volitional change, not all are. Consequently, theory needs to be contextualized. The lived experience of the body can only be understood in the context of everyday life and the constraints and possibilities inherent within. The variety of practices and the types of interpretations made of bodily signs need to be examined. For example, issues related to body maintenance are pertinent (Chapter 4), where maintenance incorporated both leaving the body alone and listening and responding to bodily signs. Clearly the contexts within which people attend to or ignore their bodies need to be well understood. Only then will we be able to develop a coherent but not deterministic picture of the relationship between the embodied individual and society. As Starobinski has argued (quoted in Frank 1991:38), '[t]he most fruitful generalisations are those arising from fairly precise studies of limited topics'.

Grounded theory provided a resolution, in the research reported here, to what were felt to be the limitations of current theorizing about the body (Chapter 2) and the neglect of men's experiences of health in qualitative social research. In both instances it provided a way of empirically approaching the lived body of the informant. The use of grounded theory does not invalidate other forms of theory or explanation. But, in dealing with issues of practice that are deeply embedded in the everyday world of informants, grounded theory provided a means of discerning and expressing what might not have been expressed before with regard to masculine knowledge about health and the body. As a method, grounded theory provides a useful common ground for health promotion – that is, it provides a means of bringing together knowledge of the practical issues that confront informants in their everyday lives with a theoretical interpretation of that experience that facilitates the identification and exploration of the shared basis of such experience.

To move to a conclusion of sorts, lay knowledge challenges the predominantly disembodied and normative nature of existing public health and health-promotion approaches to men's health. By contrast, the embodied individual perspective is complementary to analyses that focus on macrosocial concerns such as gender, race, and class, in showing how the men in this research experience and move through the circumstances of their daily existence.

In particular, this work demonstrates that informants do – with greater or lesser degrees of willingness – grapple with some of the gendered expectations of adult males sharing their particular circumstances. In this sense, informants demonstrate the communication and appreciation of shared meanings focused on lay theorizing about the body and health, whilst the analysis illuminates the embeddedness of male embodiment in the everyday worlds of informants. These informants related to each other in their recognition of the challenges and responsibilities that confront men in similar circumstances. So, for example, it may be inappropriate to seek to move them to a position of being able to relate 'more fully' to other men, at an emotional level, when they already relate at a pragmatic level. However, it may be appropriate to engage men at an emotional level at certain times and circumstances in their lives, such as bereavement or separation.

For these men there exists an inherent tension between the promotion of responsibility for individual self-care and personal responsibility derived from the functional tasks of pragmatic embodiment. Health is not central to these pragmatic tasks. In such contexts it is defined by its contingent nature. Instead, it could be suggested that its enduring presence, in the lives of these informants, is not to be found in the being and doing of their lives. Rather, it could be argued that if health has resonance for these informants it is in the various discourses of health that dissect their lives in the context of conversation, media coverage and medical surveillance: subjective, conflicting, sensationalist, impractical, impersonal and disembodied.

If health promotion is to develop the necessary understanding to support practice and policy then there is a need to consider alternative forms of explanation for commonly held ideas about the social and cultural contexts of health. That informants did theorize about the body opens up some of the spaces, silences and confusions that are concealed by overly deterministic views of the body, such as those advanced by Foucault and Douglas. Such lay perspectives also suggest the possibility of a richer interactive reading of the body.

In general, these conclusions can be cited in support of the perspective first noted by Csordas (1994) that embodiment is the personal ground of culture. This is not to argue that culture and cultural forms, such as ideal body forms, do not exist prior to individual embodiment. Rather, it is the way that individuals take up and interpret these cultural 'givens' and make them personal to themselves that is crucial. It is also to argue that informants do have some freedom to opt in and out of the various 'discourses' that confront them, for example, in the context of the well man clinic, by moving in and out of the different domains of their embodiment. Certainly, the concept of 'being in shape' can be viewed as contributing to the start of a process of attempting to express about the male body aspects of male experience not previously articulated. More importantly, it begins a process of excavating knowledge about masculine health practices in which gender relationships and public health moralities are not experienced as entirely congruent.

APPENDIX: BIOGRAPHICAL PROFILES

Accountant, 40. Born in London. Left school after A levels. Married 11 years. Girl aged 10. Owner-occupier.

Builder, 33. Born in Aberdeen. Left school at 16. Apprenticeship in building trade. Married 10 years. Separated before end of fieldwork. Girl aged 6 and boy aged 2. Owner-occupier. Cigarette smoker.

Car salesman, 36. Born in Aberdeen. Left school at 16. Married 10 years. Girl aged 9 and boy aged 6. Owner-occupier.

Catering supervisor, 32. Born in Glasgow. Did Ordinary National Diploma. Married 2 years. Boy aged 2 weeks (another due at end of fieldwork). Owner-occupier.

Communications supervisor, 33. Born in Inverness. Left college at 21. Married 12 years. Girls aged 11 and 10. Owner-occupier.

Derrick hand, 35. Born in the West Indies. Left school at 16. Married 6 years. Girl aged 4 and boy aged 3. Renting from employer. Cigarette smoker.

Drilling equipment salesman, 38. Born in rural Aberdeenshire. Left school at 16. Married 18 years. Girls aged 15 and 13. Owner-occupier. Ex-smoker.

Electrical maintenance co-ordinator, 37. Born in Stockton-on-Tees. Left school at 15. Apprenticeship. Married. Girl aged 2 and boy aged 5 days. Owner-occupier.

Electrician, 33. Born in Aberdeen. Left school at 16. Married 12 years. Boy aged 7. Rents from local authority. Cigarette smoker.

Electrician, 34. Born in Aberdeen. Left school after O levels. Common-law marriage. Three girls aged 10, 8 and 5 weeks. Owner-occupier. Cigarette smoker.

Engineer, 38. Born in Carlisle. Did Higher National Diploma followed by Open University degree. Married 15 years. Boy aged 10. Owner-occupier.

Engineer, 39. Born in Sunderland. Left school at 15. Married 16 years. Boys aged 8 and 5. Rents from local authority. Cigarette smoker.

Garage service manager, 32. Born in Aberdeen. Left school at 16. Married 10 years. Boys aged 7 and 4. Rents from local authority.

HGV driver, 31. Born in rural Aberdeenshire. Left school at 16. Married 10 years. Girl aged 7 and boy aged 5. Owner-occupier.

Industrial chemist, 38. Born in South Wales. Did Higher National Diploma. Married 21 years. Boys aged 21 and 19, girl aged 12. Owner-occupier. Ex-smoker.

Mechanic, 39. Born in rural Aberdeenshire. Left school at 15. Married 18 years. Boy aged 15 and girl aged 13. Rents from local authority.

Mechanical engineer, 37. Born in Newcastle. Did Higher National Diploma. Ex-miner. Divorced (girl aged 16 and boy aged 14) and remarried (no children). Owner-occupier.

Mechanical engineer, 40. Born in Aberdeen. Left school at 15. Served apprenticeship. Married 18 years. Boy aged 5. Owner-occupier.

Quantity surveyor, 37. Born in Aberdeen. Left school after Highers. Did apprenticeship. Married 13 years. Boy and girl twins aged 8. Owner-occupier. Ex-cigarette smoker; currently smokes eight cigars per day.

Safety engineer, 31. Born in Dundee. Left school at 16. Married (separated from wife during fieldwork). Boy aged 5 and girl aged 2. Rents from employer. Cigarette smoker.

Software engineer, 34. Born in Aberdeen. Did Higher National Diploma. Married 4 years. Boys aged 3 and 1. Owner-occupier. Ex-smoker.

Solicitor, 39. Born in Chester. Educated to degree level. Married eight years. Girl aged 4. Owner-occupier.

Teacher, 39. Born in East Yorkshire. Master's degree. Married seven years. Boy aged 9 weeks. Owner-occupier. Cigarette smoker.

Teacher, 40. Born in Widnes. Educated to degree level. Married 19 years. Boy aged 17. Owner-occupier. Ex-smoker.

Technical design manager, 37. Born in Aberdeen. Left college at 19. Falklands war veteran. Divorced (no children) and remarried. Boy aged 7 weeks. Owner-occupier. Cigarette smoker.

Technician, 32. Born in Aberdeen. Educated to degree level. Married 9 years. Two girls aged 5 and 4. Owner-occupier.

Training consultant, 40. Born in Cromarty. Left school at 15. Married 12 years. Girls aged 10 (twins) and boys aged 5 and 2. Owner-occupier. Cigarette smoker.

Unemployed roustabout, 39. Born in Aberdeen. Left school at 16. Married. Stepdaughter aged 14. Owner-occupier. Cigarette smoker.

Warehouse dispatcher, 31. Born in Aberdeen. Left school at 16. Married 6 years. Two girls aged 5 and 3. Owner-occupier.

Warehouse manager, 35. Born in Sutherland. Educated to degree level. Married ten years. Girls aged 7 and 5. Owner-occupier.

BIBLIOGRAPHY

Abel, T. (1991) Measuring health lifestyles in a comparative analysis: theoretical issues and empirical findings, *Social Science and Medicine*, 32(8): 899–908.

Abel, T. (1998) A critical approach to lifestyles and health. Paper presented to the 1st UK Health Promotion Research Conference, Edinburgh, 6–8 April.

Acheson, D. (1998) *Independent Inquiry into Inequalities in Health*. London: The Stationery Office.

Ajzen, I. and Fishbein, M. (1977) Attitude–behaviour relations: a theoretical analysis and review of empirical literature, *Psychological Bulletin*, 84: 888–918.

Alasuutari, P. (1992) *Desire and Craving: A Cultural Theory of Alcoholism*. Albany: State University of New York Press.

Alexanderson, K., Wingren, G. and Rosdahl, I. (1998) Gender analyses of medical textbooks on dermatology, epidemiology, occupational and community medicine, *Education for Health*, 11(2): 151–63.

Allat, P. (1986) Men and war: status, class and the social reproduction of masculinity, in E. Gamarnikow *et al.* (eds) *The Public and the Private*. Aldershot: Gower.

Annandale, E. and Clarke, J. (1996) What is gender? Feminist theory and the sociology of human reproduction, *Sociology of Health and Illness*, 18(1): 17–44.

Annandale, E. and Hunt, K. (1990) Masculinity, femininity and sex: an exploration of their relative contribution to explaining gender differences in health, *Sociology of Health and Illness*, 12: 24–45.

Anon. (1992) Health education research: theory and practice–future directions, *Health Education Research*, 7(1): 1–8.

Anon. (1998) Farmers' health: a neglected field, *Healthlines*, 53: 27.

Armstrong, D. (1983) *Political Anatomy of the Body: Medical Knowledge in Britain in the Twentieth Century*. Cambridge: Cambridge University Press.

Armstrong, D. (1987) Bodies of knowledge: Foucault and the problem of human anatomy, in G. Scambler (ed.) *Sociological Theory and Medical Sociology*. London: Tavistock.

Armstrong, D. (1995) The rise of surveillance medicine, *Sociology of Health and Illness*, 17(3): 393–404.

Arney, W.R. and Bergen, B.J. (1983) The anomaly, the chronic patient and the play of medical power, *Sociology of Health and Illness*, 5(1): 1–24.

Arney, W.R. and Neill, J. (1982) The location of pain in childbirth, natural childbirth and the transformation of obstetrics, *Sociology of Health and Illness*, 4(1): 1–24.

Ashenden, R., Silagy, C. and Weller, D.A. (1997) A systematic review of the effectiveness of promoting lifestyle change in general practice, *Family Practice*, 14: 160–76.

Backett, K. (1989) Public health and private lives, in C.J. Martin and D.V. McQueen (eds) *Readings for a New Public Health*. Edinburgh: Edinburgh University Press.

Backett, K. (1990) Studying health in families: a qualitative approach, in S. Cunningham-Burley and N.P. McKeganey (eds) *Readings in Medical Sociology*. London: Routledge.

Backett, K. (1992a) Taboos and excesses: lay health moralities in middle class families, *Sociology of Health and Illness*, 14(2): 255–74.

Backett, K. (1992b) The construction of health knowledge in middle class families, *Health Education Research*, 7(4): 497–507.

Backett, K. and Davison, C. (1992) Rational or reasonable? Perceptions of health at different stages of the lifecourse, *Health Education Journal*, 51(2): 55–9.

Backett, K. and Davison, C. (1995) Lifecourse and lifestyle: the social and cultural location of health behaviours, *Social Science and Medicine*, 40(5): 629–38.

Backett, K., Davison, C. and Mullen, K. (1994) The lay evaluation of health and healthy lifestyles: evidence from three studies, *British Journal of General Practice*, 44(383): 277–80.

Balarajan, R. and McDowell, M.E. (1988) Regional socioeconomic differences in mortality among men in Great Britain today, *Public Health*, 102: 33–43.

Bandura, A. (1977) *Social Learning Theory*. London: Prentice Hall.

Bauman, L.J. and Adair, E.G. (1992) The use of ethnographic interviewing to inform questionnaire construction, *Health Education Quarterly*, Spring: 9–23.

Baxter, J., Eyles, J. and Willms, D. (1992) The Hagersville tire fire: interpreting risk through a qualitative research design, *Qualitative Health Research*, 2(2): 208–37.

Beattie, A. (1991) Knowledge and control in health promotion: a test case for social policy and social theory, in J. Gabe, M. Calnan and M. Bury (eds) *The Sociology of the Health Services*. London: Routledge.

Beaune, J.-C. (1989) The classical age of automata: an impressionistic survey from the sixteenth to the nineteenth century, in M. Feher, R. Naddaff and N. Tazi (eds) *Fragments for a History of the Human Body: Part One*. New York: Zone.

Beck, U. (1992) *Risk Society: Towards a New Modernity*. London: Sage.

Becker, M. (ed.) (1974) The health belief model and personal health behaviour, *Health Education Monographs*, 2: 1–146.

Becker, P.H. (1993) Common pitfalls in published grounded theory research, *Qualitative Health Research*, 3(2): 254–60.

Bem, D.J. (1972) Self-perception theory: an alternative interpretation of cognitive dissonance phenomena, in L. Berkowitz (ed.) *Advances in Experimental Social Psychology*, Vol. 6. New York: Academic Press.

Bendelow, G. and Williams, S. (1995) Pain and the mind–body dualism: a sociological approach, *Body and Society*, 1(2): 83–104.

Berger, P.L. and Luckmann, T. (1971) *The Social Construction of Reality: A Treatise in the Sociology of Knowledge*. London: Penguin.

Blacking, J. (1977) Towards an Anthropology of the Body, in J. Blacking (ed.) *The Anthropology of the Body*. London: Academic Press.

Blaxter, M. (1990) *Health and Lifestyles*. London: Routledge/Tavistock.

Bleir, R. (1984) *Science and Gender: A Critique of Biology and Its Theories on Women*. London: Pergamon Press.

Bloor, M.J. (1978) On the analysis of observational data: a discussion of the worth and uses of inductive techniques and respondent validation, *Sociology*, 12: 545–552.

Bloor, M., Monaghan, L., Dobash, R.P. and Dobash, R.E. (1998) The body as a chemistry experiment: steroid use among South Wales bodybuilders, in Sarah Nettleton and Jonathan Watson (eds) *The Body in Everyday Life*. London and New York: Routledge.

Bourdieu, P. (1977) *Outline of a Theory of Practice*. Cambridge: Cambridge University Press.

Bourdieu, P. (1978) Sport and social class, *Social Science Information*, 17(6): 819–40.

Bourdieu, P. (1979) *Algeria 1960*. Cambridge: Cambridge University Press.

Bourdieu, P. (1984) *Distinction: A Social Critique of the Judgement of Taste* (trans. R. Nice). London: Routledge & Kegan Paul.

Bourdieu, P. (1990) *The Logic of Practice*. Cambridge: Polity Press.

Bradford, N. (1995) Is this a sick joke? *Good Housekeeping*, May.

Brandes, S. (1980) *Metaphors of Masculinity: Sex and Status in Andalusian Folklore*. Pittsburgh: University of Pennsylvania Press.

Brieger, W.R. and Kendall, C. (1992) Learning from local knowledge to improve disease surveillance: perceptions of the guinea worm illness experience, *Health Education Research*, 7(4): 471–85.

Brod, H. (ed.) (1987) *The Making of Masculinities*. Boston and London: Allen & Unwin.

Brodsky, C.M. (1954) A study of norms for body form–behaviour relationship, *Anthropological Quarterly*, 27: 91–101.

Bunton, R. (1992) More than a woolly jumper: health promotion as social regulation, *Critical Public Health*, 3: 4–11.

Bunton, R., Nettleton, S. and Burrows, R. (1995) Sociological critiques of health promotion, in R. Bunton, S. Nettleton and R. Burrows (eds) *The Sociology of Health Promotion: Critical Analyses of Consumption, Lifestyle and Risk*. London and New York: Routledge.

Bury, M. (1986) Social constructionism and the development of medical sociology, *Sociology of Health and Illness*, 8(2): 137–69.

Caplan, R. (1993) The importance of social theory for health promotion: from description to reflexivity, *Health Promotion International*, 8(2): 147–57.

Carstairs, V. and Morris, R. (1991) *Deprivation and Health in Scotland*. Aberdeen: Aberdeen University Press.

Chapman, S. (1993) Unravelling gossamer with boxing gloves: problems in explaining the decline in smoking, *British Medical Journal*, 307: 429–32.

Charmaz, K. (1990) 'Discovering' chronic illness: using grounded theory, *Social Science and Medicine*, 30(11): 1161–72.

Chernin, K. (1983) *Womansize: The Tyranny of Slenderness*. London: The Women's Press.

Chodorow, N. (1978) *The Reproduction of Mothering: Psychoanalysis and the Sociology of Gender*. London: University of California Press.

Clements, S. (1991) Male screening: time waster or life saver? *Practice Nurse*, May: 25–7.

Connell, R. (1987) *Gender and Power*. Oxford: Polity Press.

Connell, R. (1995) *Masculinities*. Oxford: Polity Press.

Cook, D.G., Morris, J.K., Walker, M. and Shaper, A.G. (1990) Consultation rates among middle aged men in general practice over three years, *British Medical Journal*, 301: 647–50.

Cornwell, J. (1984) *Hard Earned Lives: Accounts of Health and Illness from East London*. London: Tavistock.

Cowan, C.P., Cowan, P.A., Heming, G., *et al.* (1985) Transitions to parenthood: his, hers, and theirs, *Journal of Family Issues*, 6: 451–81.

Crawford, R. (1977) You are dangerous to your health: the ideology and politics of victim blaming, *International Journal of the Health Services*, 7(4): 663–80.

Crawford, R. (1984) A cultural account of health, control, release and the social body, in J.B. McKinlay (ed.) *Issues in the Political Economy of Health*. London: Tavistock.

Crossley, N. (1995) Merleau-Ponty, the elusive body and carnal sociology, *Body and Society*, 1(1): 43–64.

Csordas, T.J. (1990) Embodiment as a paradigm for anthropology, *Ethos*, 18(1): 5–47.

Csordas, T.J. (1993) Somatic modes of attention, *Cultural Anthropology*, 8(2): 135–56.

Csordas, T.J. (1994) *Embodiment and Experience: The Existential Ground of Culture and Self*. Cambridge: Cambridge University Press.

Cummings, S.R., Rubin, S.M. and Oster, G. (1989) The cost-effectiveness of counselling smokers to quit, *JAMA*, 261(1): 75–9.

Daley, J. (1998) Young men always behave badly by replacing clear academic goals with self discovery, *Daily Telegraph*, 28 April.

Danielsson, M. and Lindberg, G. (1996) Skillnader mellan mäns och kvinnors ohälsa – beständiga eller föränderliga? in P. Östlin, M. Danielsson, F. Diderichsen, A. Härenstam and G. Lindberg (eds) *Kön och ohälsa*. Lund: Studentlitteratur.

Darbyshire, P. (1987) Danger man: the traditional male lifestyle and death rates, *Nursing Times*, 83(48): 30–2.

Davison, C., Davey-Smith, G. and Frankel, S. (1991) Lay epidemiology and the prevention paradox: the implications of coronary candidacy for health education, *Sociology of Health and Illness*, 13(1): 1–19.

Davison, C., Frankel, S. and Smith, G.D. (1992) The limits of lifestyle: re-assessing 'fatalism' in the popular culture of illness prevention, *Social Science and Medicine*, 34(9): 675–85.

de Certeau, M. (1994) The practice of everyday life, in J. Storey (ed.) *Cultural Theory and Popular Culture: A Reader*. New York: Harvester Wheatsheaf.

Department of Health (DoH) (1989) *General Practice in the National Health Service: The 1990 Contract*. London: Department of Health.

Department of Health (DoH) (1992) *The Health of the Nation: A Strategy for Health in England*, Cm. 1968. London: HMSO.

Department of Health (DoH) (1993) *On the State of The Public Health*. London: HMSO.

Department of Health (DoH) (1998) *Our Healthier Nation: A Contract for Health*, Cm. 3852. London: The Stationery Office.

Desjarlais, R.R. (1992) Yolmo aesthetics of body, health and 'soul loss', *Social Science and Medicine*, 34(10): 1105–17.

d'Houtaud, A. and Field, M.G. (1984) The image of health: variations in perception by social class in a French population, *Sociology of Health and Illness*, 6(1): 30–60.

Dibiase, W.J. and Hjelle, L.A. (1968) Body-image stereotypes and body-type preferences among male college students, *Perceptual and Motor Skills*, 27: 1143–6.

Dinnerstein, D. (1976) *The Mermaid and the Minotaur: Sexual Arrangements and Human Malaise*. New York: Harper & Row.

Dong, W. and Erens, B.A. (eds) (1997) *Scottish Health Survey 1995: Volume 1*. Edinburgh: The Stationery Office.

Dong, W., Primatesta, P. and Walsh, S. (1997) Cardiovascular disease and its risk factors, in W. Dong and B.A. Erens (eds), *Scottish Health Survey 1995, Volume 1*. Edinburgh: The Stationery Office.

Douglas, M. (1975) *Implicit Meanings*. London: Routledge & Kegan Paul.

Douglas, M. (1982) *Natural Symbols: Explorations in Cosmology*. New York: Pantheon.

Douglas, M. (1988) *Purity and Danger: An Analysis of the Concepts of Pollution and Taboo*. London: Ark.

Downie, R.S., Fyfe, C. and Tannahill, A. (1990) *Health Promotion: Models and Values*. Oxford: Oxford University Press.

Downie, R.S., Tannahill, C. and Tannahill, A. (1996) *Health Promotion: Models and Values*. 2nd edition. Oxford: Oxford University Press.

Drever, F. and Bunting, J. (1997) Patterns and trends in male mortality, in F. Drever and M. Whitehead, *Health Inequalities: Decennial Supplement*. Series DS No. 15. London: The Stationery Office.

Drever, F., Whitehead, M. and Roden, M. (1996) Current patterns and trends in male mortality by social class (based on occupation), *Population Trends*, 86: 15–20.

Eales, M.J. (1989) Shame among unemployed men, *Social Science and Medicine*, 28(8): 783–9.

Easthope, A. (1986) *What a Man's Gotta Do*. London: Paladin.

Ekenstam, C. (1998) Masculinity and health. Paper presented at a course on Gender Perspectives in Research in the Socio-medical Field. Nordiska Hälsorårdshögskolan, Gothenburg.

Elam, D. (1994) *Feminism and Deconstruction*. London: Routledge.

Elias, N. (1978) *The Civilising Process, Volume 1: The History of Manners*. Oxford: Basil Blackwell. First published 1939.

Elkin, D. (1984) Teenage thinking: implications for health care, *Pediatric Nursing*, 10: 383–5.

Fabian, J. (1983) *Time and the Other*. Guildford, NY: Columbia University Press.

Fairhurst, E. (1998) 'Growing old gracefully' as opposed to 'mutton dressed as lamb': the social construction of recognising older women, in Sarah Nettleton and Jonathan Watson (eds) *The Body in Everyday Life*. London and New York: Routledge.

Falk, P. (1994) *The Consuming Body*. London: Sage.

Fareed, A. (1994) Equal rights for men, *Nursing Times*, 90(5): 26–9.

Fasteau, M.F. (1974) *The Male Machine*. New York: McGraw-Hill.

Featherstone, M. (1991) The body in consumer culture, in M. Featherstone, M. Hepworth and B.S. Turner (eds) *The Body: Social Processes and Cultural Theory*. London: Sage.

Featherstone, M. and Burrows, R. (1995) Cultures of technological embodiment: an introduction, *Body and Society*, 1(3–4): 1–20.

Featherstone, M. and Hepworth, M. (1991) The mask of ageing, in M. Featherstone, M. Hepworth and B.S. Turner (eds) *The Body: Social Processes and Cultural Theory*. London: Sage.

Featherstone, M. and Turner, B.S. (1995) Body and society: an introduction, *Body and Society*, 1(1): 1–12.

Featherstone, M., Hepworth, M. and Turner, B.S. (eds) (1991) *The Body: Social Processes and Cultural Theory*. London: Sage.

Feher, M. (1989) Introduction, in M. Feher, R. Naddaff and N. Tazi (eds) *Fragments for a History of the Human Body: Part One*. New York: Zone.

Fejes, F.J. (1992) Masculinity as fact: a review of empirical mass communication research on masculinity, in S. Craig (ed.) *Men, Masculinity, and the Media*. London: Sage.

Ferketich, S.L. and Mercer, R.T. (1989) Men's health status during pregnancy and early fatherhood, *Research in Nursing and Health*, 12: 137–48.

Fetterman, D.M. (1989) *Ethnography: Step by Step*. London: Sage.

Foucault, M. (1973) *The Birth of the Clinic*. London: Tavistock.

Foucault, M. (1979) *Discipline and Punish: The Birth of the Prison*. Harmondsworth: Penguin.

Foucault, M. (1988) Technologies of the self, in L.H. Martin, H. Gutman and P.H. Hutton (eds) *Technologies of the Self: A Seminar with Michel Foucault*. Amherst: University of Massachusetts Press.

Fox, N.J. (1993) *Postmodernism, Sociology and Health*. Buckingham: Open University Press.

Frank, A.W. (1991) For a sociology of the body: an analytical review, in M. Featherstone, M. Hepworth and B.S. Turner (eds) *The Body: Social Process and Cultural Theory*. London: Sage.

Frank, A.W. (1995) Review symposium: as much as theories can say about bodies, *Body and Society*, 1(1): 1–12.

Freund, P.E.S. (1982) *The Civilized Body: Social Domination, Control and Health*. Philadelphia: Temple University Press.

Freund, P.E.S. (1988) Bringing society into the body, *Theory and Society*, 17: 839–64.

Freund, P.E.S. (1990) The expressive body: a common ground for the sociology of emotions and health and illness, *Sociology of Health and Illness*, 12(4): 452–77.

Gabe, J. and Calnan, M. (1989) The limits of medicine: women's perceptions of medical technology, *Social Science and Medicine*, 28(2): 223–31.

Gagnon, J.H. (1974) Physical strength, once of significance, in J.H. Pleck and J. Sawyer (eds) *Men and Masculinity*. Englewood Cliffs, NJ: Prentice Hall.

Gatens, M. (1996) *Imaginary Bodies: Ethics, Power and Corporeality*. London: Routledge.

Geertz, C. (1973) *The Interpretation of Cultures*. London: Fontana.

Geertz, C. (1993) *Local Knowledge*. London: Fontana.

General Registrar Office for Scotland (GROS) (1989) *Registrar General for Scotland Annual Report 1988*. Edinburgh: HMSO.

General Registrar Office for Scotland (GROS) (1996) *Registrar General for Scotland Annual Report 1995*. Edinburgh: GROS.

Giddens, A. (1990) *The Consequences of Modernity*. Stanford, CA: Stanford University Press.

Giddens, A. (1991) *Modernity and Self-Identity: Self and Society in the Late Modern Age*. Oxford: Polity Press.

Glaser, B.G. (1978) *Theoretical Sensitivity*. Mill Valley, CA: Sociology Press.

Glaser, B.G. and Strauss, A.L. (1967) *The Discovery of Grounded Theory: Strategies for Qualitative Research*. New York: Aldine de Gruyter.

Good, B.J. (1994) *Medicine, Rationality, and Experience. An Anthropological Perspective*. Cambridge: Cambridge University Press.

Good, G.E., Dell, D.M. and Mintz, L.B. (1989) Male role and gender role conflict: relations to help seeking in men, *Journal of Counselling Psychology*, 36(3): 295–300.

Gottfried, H. (1998) Beyond patriarchy? Theorising gender and class, *Sociology*, 32(3): 451–68.

Gramsci, A. (1978) *Selections from the Prison Notebooks of Antonio Gramsci* (translated and edited by Q. Hoare and N. Smith). New York: International Publishers.

Griaule, M. (1975) *Conversations with Ogotommeli: An Introduction to Dogon Religious Ideas*. Oxford: Oxford University Press.

Ham, C., Hunter, D. and Robinson, R. (1995) Evidence based policy making, *British Medical Journal*, 310: 71–3.

Hammersley, M. and Atkinson, P. (1983) *Ethnography: Principles in Practice*. London: Tavistock.

Harris, I.M. (1995) *Messages Men Hear: Constructing Masculinities*. London: Taylor & Francis.

Hart, N. (1988) Sex, gender and survival: inequalities of life chances between European men and women, in A.J. Fox (ed.) *Inequality in Health within Europe*. Aldershot: Gower.

Hearn, J. and Morgan, D.H.J. (eds) (1990) *Men, Masculinities and Social Theory*. London: Unwin Hyman.

Heller, A. (1984) *Everyday Life*. London: Routledge & Kegan Paul.

Helman, C. (1990) *Culture, Health and Illness*. London: Wright.

Herlitzer-Allen, D.L. and Kendall, C. (1992) Explaining differences between qualitative and quantitative data: a study of chemoprophylaxis during pregnancy, *Health Education Quarterly*, 19(2): 41–55.

Herzlich, C. (1973) *Health and Illness: A Social Psychological Analysis*. London: Academic Press.

Herzlich, C. and Pierret, J. (1987) *Illness and Self in Society*. London: Johns Hopkins University Press.

Higate, P. (1998) The body resists: everyday clerking and unmilitary practice, in Sarah Nettleton and Jonathan Watson (eds) *The Body in Everyday Life*. London and New York: Routledge.

Hirschon-Weiss, C. and Wittrock, B. (1991) Social sciences and modern states, in Wagner, P., Hirschon-Weiss, C., Wittrock, B. and Wollmann, H. (eds) *Social Sciences and Modern States: National Experiences and Theoretical Crossroads*. Cambridge: Cambridge University Press.

Hochbaum, G.M., Sorenson, J.R. and Lorig, K. (1992) Theory in health education practice, *Health Education Quarterly*, 19(3): 295–313.

Hochschild, A.R. (1983) *The Managed Heart: Commercialization of Human Feeling*. London: University of California Press.

Honneth, A. and Joas, H. (1988) *Social Action and Human Nature*. Cambridge: Cambridge University Press.

Howson, A. (1996) The female body and health surveillance: cervical screening and the social construction of risk. Paper presented at Changing Organisms: Organisms and Change, Quincentenary Conference on the History of Medicine, University of Aberdeen, April.

Howson, A. (1998) Embodied obligation: the female body and health surveillance, in Sarah Nettleton and Jonathan Watson (eds) *The Body in Everyday Life*. London and New York: Routledge.

Hughes, B. (1992) Body sculpture: eating for the sake of appearance. Paper presented at the Theory, Culture and Society 10th Anniversary Conference, Seven Springs, PA, August.

Hunt, K., Ford, G., Harkins, L. and Wyke, S. (1999) Are women more ready to consult than men? Gender differences in family practitioner consultation for common chronic conditions, *Journal of Health Service Research and Policy*, 4(2): 96–100.

Hunt, S.M. and Macleod, M. (1987) Health and behavioural change: some lay perspectives, *Community Medicine*, 9(1): 68–76.

Hurst, P. and Wolley, P. (1982) *Social Relations and Human Attributes*. London: Tavistock.

Hutton, P.H. (1988) Foucault, Freud, and the technologies of the self, in L.H. Martin, H. Gutman, P.H. Hutton (eds) *Technologies of the Self: A Seminar with Michel Foucault*. Amherst: University of Massachusetts Press.

Illich, I. (1986) Body history, *The Lancet*, 2(8519): 1325–7.

Information and Statistics Division Scotland (1998a) *Cancer Registration Statistics Scotland 1986–1995*. Edinburgh: Scottish Cancer Intelligence Unit.

Information and Statistics Division Scotland (1998b) *Scottish Health Statistics 1997*. Edinburgh: Common Services Agency.

Jack, M.S. (1989) Personal fable: a potential explanation for risk-taking behaviour in adolescents, *Journal of Paediatric Nursing*, 4: 334–8.

Jackson, C. (1991) Men's health: opening the floodgates, *Health Visitor*, 64(8): 265–6.

Jagger, A.M. (1983) *Feminist Politics and Human Nature*. London: Harvester Press.

Johnson, M. (1987) *The Body in the Mind: The Bodily Basis of Meaning, Imagination, and Reason*. London: University of Chicago Press.

Jordonova, L. (1989) *Sexual Visions: Images of Gender in Science and Medicine between the Eighteenth and Twentieth Centuries*. London and New York: Harvester Wheatsheaf.

Julian, T., McKenry, P.C. and McKelvey, M.W. (1992) Components of men's well-being at midlife, *Mental Health Nursing*, 13: 285–99.

Jung, H.Y. (1976) Embodiment and political action, *Philosophy Forum*, 14: 367–88.

Kannel, W.B. and Gordon, T. (1974) *The Framingham Study: An Epidemiological Investigation of Cardiovascular Disease*. Washington, DC: National Institutes of Health.

Kappeler, S. (1994/5) From sexual politics to body politics, *Trouble and Strife*, (Winter): 73–9.

Keller, E.F. (1985) *Reflections on Gender and Science*. London: Yale University Press.

Kelly, M. (1992) *Colitis*. London: Routledge.

Kelly, M.P. (1989) Some problems with health promotion research, *Health Promotion*, 4: 317–30.

Kelly, M.P., Watson, J.M. and Tannahill, C. (no date) Loosening the chains: phenomenology and participatory health promotion. Unpublished working paper.

Kimmel, M.S. (1987) Rethinking masculinity: new directions in research, in M.S. Kimmel (ed.) *Changing Men: New Directions in Research on Men and Masculinity*. London: Sage.

Klein, H. (1991) Couvade syndrome – male counterpart to pregnancy, *International Journal of Psychiatry in Medicine*, 21(1): 57–69.

Kleinman, A. (1988) *The Illness Narratives: Suffering, Healing and the Human Condition*. New York: Basic.

Kreitman, N., Carstairs, V. and Duffy, J. (1991) Association of age and social class with suicide among men in Great Britain, *Journal of Epidemiology and Community Health*, 45(3): 195–202.

Kristiansen, C.M. (1989) Gender differences in the meaning of 'health', *Social Behaviour*, 4: 185–8.

Kroker, A. and Kroker, M. (1988) Theses on the disappearing body in the hyper-modern condition, in A. Kroker and M. Kroker (eds) *Body Invaders: Sexuality and the Postmodern Condition*. Basingstoke: Macmillan.

Lakoff, G. (1987) *Women, Fire, and Dangerous Things: What Categories Reveal about the Mind*. London: University of Chicago Press.

Laqueur, T. (1990) *Making Sex: Body and Gender from the Greeks to Freud*. London: Harvard University Press.

Lawler, J. (1991) *Behind the Screens: Nursing, Somology, and the Problem of the Body*. Edinburgh: Churchill Livingstone.

Lawrence, S.C. and Bendixen, K. (1992) His and hers: male and female anatomy in anatomy texts for U.S. medical students, *Social Science and Medicine*, 35(7): 925–34.

Leder, D. (1990) Flesh and blood: a proposed supplement to Merleau-Ponty, *Human Studies*, 13: 209–19.

Leder, D. (1992) 'Introduction', in D. Leder (ed.) *The Body in Medical Thought and Practice*. London: Kluwer Academic.

Leininger, M. (1985) Ethnography and ethnonursing: models and modes of qualitative analysis, in M. Leininger (ed.) *Qualitative Research Methods in Nursing*. London: Grune & Stratton.

Levinson, D. (1978) *The Seasons of a Man's Life*. New York: Pantheon.

Lévi-Strauss, C. (1981) *The Savage Mind*. London: Weidenfeld and Nicolson.

Lichtenstein, M.J., Shipley, M.J. and Rose, G. (1985) Systolic and diastolic blood pressures as predictors of coronary heart disease mortality in the Whitehall study, *British Medical Journal*, 291: 243–5.

Lloyd, T. (1996) *Men's Health Review*. London: Royal College of Nursing.

Long, A.F. (1993) Understanding health and disease: towards a knowledge base for public health action. Report of a workshop held at the Nuffield Institute for Health, University of Leeds, October.

Lupton, D. (1993) Risk as moral danger: the social and political functions of risk discourse in public health, *International Journal of the Health Services*, 23(3): 425–35.

Lupton, D. (1994) Consumerism, commodity culture and health promotion, *Health Promotion International*, 9: 111–18.

Lupton, D. (1995) *The Imperative of Health: Public Health and the Regulated Body*. London: Sage.

Lupton, D. (1998) Going with the flow: some central discourses in conceptualising and articulating the embodiment of emotional states, in Sarah Nettleton and Jonathan Watson (eds) *The Body in Everyday Life*. London: Routledge.

Lützén, K. and Nordin, C. (1993) Benevolence, a central moral concept derived from a grounded theory study of nursing decision making in psychiatric settings, *Journal of Advanced Nursing*, 18: 1106–11.

MacInnes, A. and Milburn, K. (1994) Belief systems and social circumstances influencing the health choices of people in Lochaber, *Health Education Journal*, 53(1): 58–72.

Macintyre, S. (1997) The Black report and beyond: what are the issues? *Social Science and Medicine*, 44(6): 723–45.

MacKenzie, J.M. (1987) The imperial pioneer and hunter and the British masculine stereotype in late Victorian and Edwardian times, in J.A. Mangan and J. Walvin (eds) (1987) *Manliness and Morality: Middle-Class in Britain and America, 1800–1940*. Manchester: Manchester University Press.

MacPherson, I.A. and Williamson, P.J. (1992) 'Not quite what I meant!' – Techniques of respondent validation, *Research, Policy and Planning*, 10(1): 10–13.

Mahoney, E.R. (1974) Body-cathexis and self-esteem: the importance of subjective importance, *Journal of Psychology*, 88: 27–30.

Mangan, J.A. and Walvin, J. (eds) (1987) *Manliness and Morality: Middle-Class in Britain and America, 1800–1940*. Manchester: Manchester University Press.

Martin, E. (1989) *The Woman in the Body: A Cultural Analysis of Reproduction*. Milton Keynes: Open University Press.

Martin, E. (1994) *Flexible Bodies: The Role of Immunity in American Culture from the Days of Polio to the age of AIDS.* Boston, MA: Beacon Press.

Mauss, M. (1989) A category of the human mind: the notion of the person; the notion of the self (trans. W.D. Halls), in M. Carrithers, S. Collins and S. Lukes (eds) *The Category of the Person: Anthropology, Philosophy, History.* Cambridge: Cambridge University Press.

Mayer, R.R. (1972) *Social Planning and Social Change.* Englewood Cliffs, NJ: Prentice Hall.

Mayo, K. (1992) Physical activity practices among American black working women, *Qualitative Health Research*, 2(3): 318–33.

McCarron, P.G., Davey Smith, G. and Womersley, J.J. (1994) Deprivation and mortality in Glasgow: changes from 1980 to 1992, *British Medical Journal*, 309(6967): 1481–2.

McCracken, G. (1988) *The Long Interview.* London: Sage.

McKeganey, N.P. and Bloor, M.J. (1981) On the retrieval of sociological descriptions: respondent validation and the critical case of ethnomethodology, *International Journal of Sociology and Social Policy*, 1(3): 58–69.

McLoone, P. (1996) Suicide and deprivation in Scotland, *British Medical Journal*, 312(7030): 521–88.

McLoone, P. and Boddy, F.A. (1994) Deprivation and mortality in Scotland, 1981 and 1991, *British Medical Journal*, 309(6967): 1465–70.

McNay, L. (1992) *Foucault and Feminism: Power, Gender and the Self.* London: Polity Press.

Mendelsohn, K., Nieman, L., Isaacs, K., Lee, S. and Levison, S. (1994) Sex and gender bias in anatomy and physical diagnosis text illustrations, *Journal of the American Medical Association*, 276: 1267–70.

Merleau-Ponty, M. (1962) *Phenomenology of Perception*, trans. C. Smith. London: Routledge & Kegan Paul.

Merleau-Ponty, M. (1968) *The Visible and the Invisible*, trans. Alphonso Lingis. Evanston, IL: Northwestern University Press.

Mishkind, M.E., Rodin, J., Silberstein, L.R. and Striegel-Moore, R.H. (1987) The embodiment of masculinity: cultural, psychological and behavioural dimensions, in M.S. Kimmel (ed.) *Changing Men: New Directions in Research on Men and Masculinity.* London: Sage.

Montemayor, R. (1978) Men and their bodies: the relationship between body type and behaviour, *Journal of Social Issues*, 34: 48–64.

Mortimer, J.T. (1988) Work experience and psychological change throughout the lifecourse, in M.W. Riley (ed.) *Social Structures and Human Lives.* London: Sage.

Mullen, K. (1992) A question of balance: health behaviour and work context among male Glaswegians, *Sociology of Health and Illness*, 14(1): 73–97.

Mullen, K. (1993) *A Healthy Balance: Glaswegian Men Talking about Health, Tobacco and Alcohol.* Aldershot: Avebury.

Mullen, P.J. and Reynolds, R. (1978) The potential of grounded theory for health education research, *Health Education Monographs*, 6: 208–303.

Munley, G. and McGloughlin, A. (1998) Accounting for gender differences in health check attendance intention and behaviour in young adults. Paper presented to the 1st UK Health Promotion Research Conference, Edinburgh, 6–8 April.

Murphy, R.F. (1987) *The Body Silent*. New York: Henry Holt & Company.

Naidoo, J. and Daykin, N. (1995) Feminist critiques of health promotion, in R. Bunton, S. Nettleton and R. Burrows (eds) *The Sociology of Health Promotion: Critical Analyses of Consumption, Lifestyle and Risk*. London and New York: Routledge.

National Audit Office (1989) *Coronary Heart Disease*. London: NAO.

Nead, L. (1992) Framing and freeing: utopias of the female body, *Radical Philosophy*, 60(Spring): 12–15.

Nettleton, S. (1988) Protecting a vulnerable margin: towards an analysis of how the mouth came to be separated from the body, *Sociology of Health and Illness*, 10(2): 156–69.

Nettleton, S. (1989) Power and pain: the location of pain and fear in dentistry and the creation of the dental subject, *Social Science and Medicine*, 29(10): 1183–90.

Nettleton, S. and Watson, J. (1998a) The body in everyday life: an introduction, in S. Nettleton and J. Watson (eds) *The Body in Everyday Life*. London and New York: Routledge.

Nettleton, S. and Watson, J. (eds) (1998b) *The Body in Everyday Life*. London and New York: Routledge.

Nutbeam D. (1998) *Health Promotion Glossary*. Geneva: World Health Organization.

Oakley, A. (1972) *Sex, Gender and Society*. London: Maurice Temple Smith.

Office for National Statistics (1997) *Living in Britain: Results from the 1995 General Household Survey*. London: The Stationery Office.

Office for National Statistics (1998) *Living in Britain: Results from the 1996 General Household Survey*. London: The Stationery Office.

Orbach, S. (1988) *Fat is a Feminist Issue*. London: Arrow.

Ortner, S.B. (1984) Theory in anthropology since the sixties, *Comparative Studies in Society and Health*, 26(1): 126–66.

Park, R.J. (1987) Biological thought, athletics and the formation of a 'man of character': 1830–1900, in J.A. Mangan and J. Walvin (eds) *Manliness and Morality: Middle-class Masculinity in Britain and America 1800–1940*. Manchester: Manchester University Press.

Petersen, A. (1997) Risk, governance and the new public health, in A. Petersen and R. Bunton (eds) *Foucault, Health and Medicine*. London: Routledge.

Petersen, A. and Bunton, R. (eds) (1997) *Foucault, Health and Medicine*. London: Routledge.

Pill, R. and Stott, N.C. (1985) Preventive procedures and practices among working class women: new data and fresh insights, *Social Science and Medicine*, 21(9): 975–83.

Pill, R. and Stott, N.C. (1987) The stereotype of working class fatalism and the challenge for primary care health promotion, *Health Education Research*, 2(2): 105–14.

Platt, S. (1984) Unemployment and suicidal behaviour: a review of the literature, *Social Science and Medicine*, 19(2): 93–115.

Pleck, J. (1981) *The Myth of Masculinity*. London: MIT Press.

Pocock, S.J., Shaper, A.G., Cook, D.G., Phillips, A.N. and Walker, M. (1987) Social class differences in ischaemic heart disease in British men, *Lancet*, 2(8552): 197–201.

Popay, J. and Williams, G. (1996) Public health research and lay knowledge, *Social Science and Medicine*, 42(5): 759–68.

Popay, J., Williams, G., Thomas, C. and Gatrell, T. (1998) Theorising inequalities in health: the place of lay knowledge, *Sociology of Health and Illness*, 20(5): 619–44.

Prendegast, S. (1992) *This is the Time to Grow Up*. Cambridge: Health Promotion Research Trust.

Puska, P., Salonen, J.T., Nissinen, A. *et al.* (1983) Change in risk factors for coronary heart disease during ten years of a community intervention programme (North Karelia Project), *British Medical Journal*, 287: 1840–4.

Research & Evaluation Division (1996) How effective are effectiveness reviews? *Health Education Journal*, 55: 359–62.

Ricoeur, P. (1969) *The Symbolism of Evil*. London: Beacon.

Riley, M.W. (1988) On the significance of age in sociology, in M.W. Riley (ed.) *Social Structures and Human Lives*. London: Sage.

Roberson, M.H.B. (1992) The meaning of compliance: patient perspectives, *Qualitative Health Research*, 2(1): 7–26.

Robertson, S. (1995) Men's health promotion in the UK: a hidden problem, *British Journal of Nursing*, 4(7): 382, 399–401.

Rogers, A., Popay, J., Williams, G. and Latham, M. (1997) *Inequalities in Health and Health Promotion: Insights from the Qualitative Research Literature*. London: Health Education Authority.

Rogers, E.M. and Shoemaker, F.F. (1971) *Communication of Innovations: A Cross Cultural Approach*, 2nd edn. New York: Free Press.

Rossi, A. (ed.) (1985) *Gender and the Life Course*. New York: Aldine.

Royal College of General Practitioners (1986) *Alcohol – A Balanced View*. London: Royal College of General Practitioners.

Royal College of Psychiatrists (1986) *Alcohol: Our Favourite Drug*. London: Tavistock.

Ruwaard, D. and Kramers, P.G.N. (eds) (1998) *Public Health Status and Forecasts 1997: Health, Prevention and Health Care in the Netherlands until 2015*. The Hague: National Institute of Public Health and the Environment (RIVM).

Ryn, M. van and Heaney, C.A. (1992) What's the use of theory? *Health Education Quarterly*, 19(3): 315–30.

Sabo, D. and Gordon, D.F. (eds) (1995) *Men's Health and Illness: Gender, Power and the Body*. Thousand Oaks, CA: Sage.

Saco, D. (1992) Masculinity as signs: poststructuralist feminist approaches to the study of gender, in S. Craig (ed.) *Men, Masculinity and the Media*. London: Sage.

Saltonstall, R. (1993) Healthy bodies – social bodies: men's and women's concepts and practices of health in everyday life, *Social Science and Medicine*, 36(1): 7–14.

Sawday, J. (1995) *The Body Emblazoned: Dissection and the Human Body in Renaissance Culture*. London: Routledge.

Sayers, J. (1986) *Sexual Contradictions: Psychology, Psychoanalysis and Feminism*. London: Tavistock.

Scheper-Hughes, N. and Lock, M.M. (1987) The mindful body: a prolegomenon to future work in medical anthropology, *Medical Anthropology Quarterly*, 1(1): 6–41.

Schwartz, H. (1986) *Never Satisfied: A Cultural History of Diets, Fantasies and Fat.* London: Free Press.

Scott, R.A. (1969) *The Making of Blind Men.* New York: Russell Sage Foundation.

Scott, S. and Morgan, D. (eds) (1993) *Body Matters: Essays on the Sociology of the Body,* London: Falmer Press.

Scottish Office Department of Health (SODoH) (1992) *Scotland's Health: A Challenge to Us All.* Edinburgh: HMSO.

Scottish Office Department of Health (SODoH) (1997) *Health in Scotland.* Edinburgh: HMSO.

Scottish Office Department of Health (SODoH) (1998a) *1997 Health in Scotland.* Edinburgh: HMSO.

Scottish Office Department of Health (SODoH) (1998b) *Towards a Healthier Scotland,* Cm. 4269. Edinburgh: The Stationery Office.

Scottish Office Department of Health, Public Health Policy Unit (SODoH, PHPU) (1996) *Coronary Heart Disease in Scotland: Report of a Policy Review.* Edinburgh: Scottish Office DoH Public Health Policy Unit.

Scottish Office Home and Health Department (SOHHD) (1989) *Scottish Health Authorities: Review of Priorities for the Eighties and Nineties (SHARPEN).* Edinburgh: HMSO.

Scottish Office Home and Health Department (SOHHD) (1991) *Health Education in Scotland: A National Policy Statement.* Edinburgh: HMSO.

Secker, J., Wimbush, E., Watson, J. and Milburn, K. (1995) Qualitative research methods in health promotion research: some criteria for quality, *Health Education Journal*, 54: 74–87.

Segal, L. (1990) *Slow Motion: Changing Masculinities, Changing Men.* London: Virago.

Seidal, J.V., Kjolseth, R. and Seymour, E. (1988) *The Ethnograph: A User's Guide.* Littleton, CO: Qualis Research Associates.

Seidler, Vic (1997) *Man Enough: Embodying Masculinities.* London: Sage.

Shaper, A.G., Pocock, S.J., Walker, M., Cohen, N.M., Wale, C.J. and Thomson, A.G. (1981) British regional heart study: cardiovascular risk factors in middle-aged men in 24 towns, *British Medical Journal*, 283: 179–86.

Shakespeare, T. (1998) Social construction as a rhetorical strategy, in I. Velody and R. Williams (eds) *The Politics of Constructionism.* London: Sage.

Shakespeare, T. and Watson, N. (1995) Habeamus corpus? Sociology of the body and the issue of impairment. Paper presented at 'Changing Organisms: Organisms and Change' Quincentennial Conference on the History of Medicine, University of Aberdeen, July.

Shaper, A.G., Pocock, S.J., Phillips, A.N. and Walker, M. (1986) Identifying men at high risk of heart attacks: strategy for use in general practice, *British Medical Journal*, 293: 474–9.

Shilling, C. (1991) Educating the body: physical capital and the production of social inequalities, *Sociology*, 25(4): 653–72.

Shilling, C. (1993) *The Body and Social Theory.* London: Sage.

Silverman, D. (1985) *Qualitative Methodology and Sociology.* Aldershot: Gower.

Silverman, D. (1987) *Communication and Medical Practice: Social Relations in the Clinic.* London: Sage.

Skorupski, J. (1976) *Symbol and Theory.* Cambridge: Cambridge University Press.

Somers, M.R. (1994) The narrative constitution of identity: a relational and network approach, *Theory and Society*, 23: 605–49.

Speller V., Learmonth A. and Harrison D. (1997) The search for evidence of effective health promotion, *British Medical Journal*, 315: 361–3.

Spradley, J. (1979) *The Ethnographic Interview*. New York: Holt, Rinehart & Winston.

Springhall, J. (1987) Building character in the British boy: the attempt to extend Christian manliness to working-class adolescents, 1880–1914, in J.A. Mangan and J. Walvin (eds) *Manliness and Morality: Middle-Class in Britain and America, 1800–1940*. Manchester: Manchester University Press.

Stafford, B. (1995) Fit or misfit, or bodies without change. Paper presented to the 'Changing Organisms: Organisms and Change' Quincentennial Conference on the History of Medicine, University of Aberdeen, July.

Standing Medical Advisory Committee (1990) *Blood Cholesterol Testing. The Cost Effectiveness of Opportunistic Testing*. London: HMSO.

Stern, P.N. (1985) Using grounded theory method in nursing research, in M. Leininger (ed.) *Qualitative Research Methods in Nursing*. London: Grune & Stratton.

Stern, P.N. (ed.) (1986) *Women, Health and Culture*. London: Hemisphere.

Stern, P.N. and Pyles, S.H. (1986) Using grounded theory methodology to study women's culturally-based decisions about health, in P.N. Stern (ed.) *Women, Health and Culture*. London: Hemisphere.

Strong, P. (1986) Sociological imperialism and the profession of medicine, *Social Science and Medicine*, 13A: 199–215.

Sugerman, A.A. and Haronian, F. (1964) Body type and sophistication of body concept, *Journal of Personality*, 32: 380–94.

Tannahill, A. (1994) *Health Education and Health Promotion: From Priorities to Programmes*. Edinburgh: Health Education Board for Scotland.

Tannahill, A. (1998) The Scottish green paper: beyond a healthy mind in a healthy body, *Journal of Public Health Medicine*, 20(3): 249–52.

Tesch, R. (1990) *Qualitative Research: Analysis Types and Software Tools*. London: Falmer Press.

Thorogood, N. (1992) What is the relevance of sociology for health promotion? in R. Bunton and G. Macdonald (eds) *Health Promotion: Disciplines and Diversity*. London: Routledge.

Tones, B.K. (1982) Beyond the consultation: the health education role of the primary health care team. Paper presented to the MSD Foundation Colloquium on the Consultation, London, March.

Tones, K. (1986) Health education and the ideology of health promotion: a review of alternative approaches, Health Education Research, 1: 3–12.

Tones, K. (1987) Devising strategies for preventing drug misuse: the role of the health action model, *Health Education Research*, 2: 305–17.

Tones, K. (1997) Beyond the randomised outcome trial: a case for judicial review, *Health Education Research*, 12(2): i–iv.

Tones, K., Tilford, S. and Anderson, Y. (1990) *Health Education: Effectiveness and Efficiency*. London: Chapman & Hall.

Trevelyan, J. (1989) Well men, *Nursing Times*, 85(12): 46–7.

Tunstall-Pedoe, H. (1989) Who is for cholesterol testing? *British Medical Journal*, 298: 1593–4.

Tunstall-Pedoe, H., Smith, W.C.S., Crombie, I.K. and Tavendale, R. (1989) Coronary risk factor and lifestyle variation across Scotland: results from the Scottish Heart Health study, *Scottish Medical Journal*, 34: 556–60.

Turner, B.S. (1984) *The Body and Society: Explorations in Social Theory*. Oxford: Basil Blackwell.

Turner, B.S. (1992) *Regulating Bodies: Essays in Medical Sociology*. London: Routledge.

Turner, T. (1980) The social skin, in J. Cherfas and R. Lewin (eds) *Not Work Alone: A Cross Cultural View of Activities Superfluous to Survival*. London: Temple-Smith.

Turner, V.W. (1960) Muchona the hornet, interpreter of religion (Northern Rhodesia), in J.B. Casagrande (ed.) *In the Company of Man: Twenty Portraits by Anthropologists*. New York: Harper & Row.

Turner, V.W. (1969) *The Ritual Process*. London: Aldine.

Van Buynder, P.G. and Smith, J.M. (1995) Mortality, myth, or mateship gone mad: the crisis in men's health, *Health Promotion Journal of Australia*, 5(3): 9–11.

Van Gennep, A. (1960) *The Rites of Passage*. London: Routledge & Kegan Paul.

Variations Sub-Group of the Chief Medical Officers Health of the Nation Working Group (1996) *Variations in Health: What Can the Department of Health and the NHS do?* London: Department of Health.

Vaskilampi, T. (1981) Sociological aspects of community-based health intervention programmes: the North Karelia project as an example, *Revue Épidémiologie et Santé Publique*, 29: 187–97.

Verbrugge, L.M. (1985) Gender and health: an update on hypotheses and evidence, *Journal of Health and Social Behaviour*, 26: 156–82.

Verbrugge, L.M. (1989) The twain meet: empirical explanations of sex differences in health and mortality, *Journal of Health and Social Behaviour*, 30(September): 282–304.

Wacquant, L.J.D. (1995) Pugs at work: bodily capital and bodily labour among professional boxers, *Body and Society*, 1(1): 65–93.

Wallston, K.A., Wallston, B.S. and Devellis, R. (1978) Development of the multidimensional health locus of control (MHLC) scales, *Health Education Monographs*, 6: 160–70.

Watson, J. (1998) Running around like a lunatic: Colin's body and the case of male embodiment, in S. Nettleton and J. Watson (eds) *The Body in Everyday Life*. London and New York: Routledge.

Watson, J., Cunningham-Burley, S., Watson, N. and Milburn, K. (1996) Lay theorizing about 'the body' and implications for health promotion, *Health Education Research*, 11(2): 161–72.

Wax, R.H. (1971) *Doing Fieldwork: Warnings and Advice*. London: Chicago University Press.

WHO European Collaborative Group (1986) European trial of multifactorial prevention of coronary heart disease: final report of the 6-year results, *Lancet*, 1(8486): 869–72.

Wight, D. (1993) *Workers or Wasters: Masculine Responsibility, Consumption and Employment in Central Scotland*. Edinburgh: Edinburgh University Press.

Wilkinson, R.G. (1997) Socioeconomic determinants of health. Health inequalities: relative or absolute material standards? *British Medical Journal*, 314: 591–5.

Williams, A. (1987) Screening for risk of CHD: is it a wise use of resources? in M. Oliver, M. Ashley-Miller and D. Wood, *Screening for Risk of CHD*. Chichester: John Wiley & Sons.

Williams, R. (1990) *A Protestant Legacy: Attitudes to Death and Illness among Older Aberdonians*. Oxford: Clarendon Press.

Williams, S.J. and Bendelow, G. (1998) *Embodying Sociology: Critical Perspectives on the Dualist Legacies*. London: Routledge.

Williams, S.J. and Calnan, M. (1996) The 'limits' of medicalization? Modern medicine and the lay populace in 'late' modernity, *Social Science and Medicine*, 42(12): 1609–20.

Willott, S. and Griffin, C. (1997) 'Wham bam, am I a man?': unemployed men talk about masculinities, *Feminism and Psychology*, 7(1): 107–28.

Woods, N.F., Laffrey, S., Duffy, M. *et al.* (1988) Being healthy: women's images, *Advanced Nursing Science*, 11(1): 36–46.

Working Group on Prevention and Health Promotion (1989) *Prevention of Coronary Heart Disease in Scotland*. Edinburgh: Scottish Home and Health Department.

World Health Organization (WHO) (1986) *Ottawa Charter for Health Promotion*. Geneva: World Health Organization.

World Health Organization (WHO) (1994) *World Health Statistics Annual*. Geneva: WHO.

World Health Organization (WHO) (1998a) *Life in the 21st Century: A Vision for All* (World Health Report). Geneva: World Health Organization.

World Health Organization (WHO) (1998b) *Gender and Health*, Technical Paper. Geneva: World Health Organization.

Wyke, S., Hunt, K. and Ford, G. (1998) Gender differences in consulting a general practitioner for common symptoms of minor illness, *Social Science and Medicine*, 46: 901–6.

Young, I.M. (1980) Throwing like a girl: a phenomenology of feminine body comportment, motility and spatiality, *Human Studies*, 3: 137–56.

Young, K. (1989) Disembodiment: the phenomenology of the body in medical examinations, *Semotica*, 73(1/2): 43–66.

Zola, I.K. (1982) *Missing Pieces: A Chronicle of Living with Disability*. Philadelphia: Temple University Press.

INDEX